PICNICS

Delicious Food for Moveable Feasts

PICNICS

Delicious Food for Moveable Feasts

Louise Pickford

JG PRESS

A SALAMANDER BOOK

Published in the USA in 1996 by JG Press
Distributed by World Publications, Inc.

The JG Press imprint is a trademark of
JG Press, Inc.
455 Somerset Avenue
North Dighton, MA 02764

ISBN 1-57215-191-9

Copyright © Salamander Books Ltd 1992, 1996

Editor: ANNE MCDOWALL
Designer: TIM SCOTT
Photographer: MARIE-LOUISE AVERY
Home Economist: LOUISE PICKFORD
Stylist: LUCY ELWORTHY
Illustrator: ORIOL BATH
Typesetting: SX COMPOSING LTD.
Color reproduction: SCANTRANS PTE. LTD.

All correspondence concerning the content
of this volume should be addressed to
Salamander Books Ltd.
129–137 York Way, London
N7 9LG, United Kingdom

This book may not be sold outside
the United States of America.

Printed in Singapore

CONTENTS

INTRODUCTION   6

PICNICS TO GO   8

FOOD WITH FIRE   34

MOVEABLE FEASTS   60

DINING ALFRESCO   86

INDEX   110

ACKNOWLEDGMENTS   112

~

INTRODUCTION

Eating outdoors is one of life's great pleasures. At the beach, the aroma of grilling food mingles with the sea air. Or there's the woody scent of the park and the light bouquet of trees and flowers in the backyard. Just about any outdoor spot you can tote a basket to will naturally add its own 'seasoning' to the meal – and a special touch to the occasion. Occasions for outdoor dining are myriad, whether for birthdays, baseball games, dinner parties – not to mention simply taking time out to celebrate nature with someone special.

PICNICS complements American 'pioneer' spirit with European style, providing elegant recipes easily prepared for any excursion, whether on a picnic, at a barbecue, or outdoors at home.

Picnics to Go comprises quick and easy recipes for informal, spur-of-the-moment meals, all with lots of flavor and a little more dash than mere cold-cut sandwiches or frankfurters. Moveable Feasts offers a chance to make picnic meals more elaborate with a little extra time and effort, yet still allows easy transportation.

With the same take on simplicity with elegance, Food with Fire is full of tantalizing dishes specifically meant for cooking over a grill or campfire. Barbecues warm the heart no matter what the season and these recipes will lend great flavor to the fun.

Dining Alfresco is for truly special occasions and the recipes here are
ideal for outdoor dinner parties at home (when you will still have
access to the kitchen). Much of the meal is prepared in advance so
you're free to relax with guests and enjoy the day.

No matter what the occasion or how each recipe is prepared, each
chapter provides tips on packing dishes for carrying, serving
suggestions, even advice on choosing china and other dinnerware.
Here are a few basic tips and reminders for dining outdoors:

Food safety Reusable plastic ice packs placed in the cooler are invaluable for keeping foods cold, particularly dairy and egg products. An ordinary thermos is great for keeping foods hot, especially soups. Remember not to serve food on the same plates on which they were prepared, unless they have been thoroughly washed.

Packing food Coolers are the most practical, convenient, and readily found containers for food to be carried outdoors. They ensure proper temperatures, keep food out of direct sunlight, and are available in grocery, department, and sporting goods stores. A pretty wicker picnic hamper or basket may be used for shorter trips. They are generally available in specialty shops and finer department stores.

Last-minute preparations Before setting out on your picnic or just before guests arrive at home, give your basket or dining table a once-over to be sure that you have everything you need, such as silverware, cutlery, even a cork screw. For picnics, don't forget a trash bag for cleaning up.

Notes

° 1 tbsp chopped fresh herbs = 1 tsp dried herbs.

° All recipes serve 6 unless otherwise stated.

PICNICS TO GO

When it comes to picnicking, there's nothing quite as inspiring as awakening to a gloriously sunny day. To get out of the kitchen and into the fresh air as soon as possible is just what the recipes in this chapter are meant to allow you to do.

These tasty dishes are not only quick and easy to prepare, they also use staple ingredients commonly kept in the cupboard or refrigerator, or easily found at the grocery store. Alternatives are suggested for ingredients that may be harder to find.

Most of these recipes can be ready within half an hour, and tips are often given in the introductions for the most suitable method of packing. For maximum convenience, plastic and paper tableware are available in a diversity of prints and qualities, and they pack up in a snap. In the interest of the environment, however, keep in mind that all dishes here will fit into a cooler or knapsack, along with regular dinnerware from home.

Ideal for the traditional picnic, whether at the park or the beach, they may also be the sumptuous highlight of an all-day hike, or an otherwise ho-hum outdoor lunch break. All of these dishes will add a little more pizazz to the occasion than the usual cold-cut sandwich.

CONTENTS

Chilled melon and mint soup
Summer avocado dip with crudités 10

Smoked salmon 'sausages'
Iced cucumber soup 12

Curried eggs
Eggplant pâté 14

Bacon and mushroom pie
Cos salad with blue brie dressing...16

Spinach tortilla
Carrot and zucchini salad 18

Chicken liver pâté
Sausage, bacon and apricot kabobs 20

Pasta salad with tuna sauce
Watercress and salmon rolls 22

Salade Niçoise
Leeks à la Grecque 24

Sicilian potato salad
Three bean salad 26

Strawberry cheese with shortbread
Summer berry fool..28

Ricotta, nut and honey cheese
Refrigerator cake...30

Sparkling fruit cup
Orchard bloom
Pink peril..32

CHILLED MELON & MINT SOUP

~

If you have room in your picnic hamper, take along the hollowed-out melon shells. They make excellent and attractive soup bowls.

6 SMALL CANTALOUPE MELONS

2 SCALLIONS, TRIMMED AND CHOPPED

2 TABLESPOONS CHOPPED MINT

4 TABLESPOONS WHITE WINE

¾ TEASPOON GROUND GINGER

2 CUPS YOGURT

SALT AND PEPPER

TO GARNISH

MINT SPRIGS

◇ Slice the tops from the melons and reserve. Scoop out the seeds into a strainer over a bowl to catch the juices. Discard the seeds but reserve the juice.

◇ Scoop out the melon flesh and purée with the scallion, mint, wine and ginger in a food processor or blender. Stir in the yogurt and up to 1¼ cups of reserved juice. Season to taste.

◇ Pour into a plastic container and chill until required.

◇ Transport the soup in the container, in a cooler, and serve chilled in the melon shells, if wished. Garnish with mint sprigs.

SUMMER AVOCADO DIP WITH CRUDITÉS

~

This is a fresh-tasting avocado dip with cottage cheese, mint and just enough lemon juice to add a light tang. Cover the surface of the dip with plastic wrap to prevent the avocado from discoloring.

1 LARGE RIPE AVOCADO

1 TABLESPOON LEMON JUICE

2 TABLESPOONS CHOPPED FRESH MINT

⅓ CUP COTTAGE CHEESE

1 SMALL RED SWEET PEPPER, SEEDED AND FINELY CHOPPED

SALT AND PEPPER

CRUDITÉS

FENNEL, LEEKS, LETTUCE HEARTS, RADISHES, TOMATOES, RED AND GREEN GRAPES

◇ Halve and peel the avocado, discarding the pit. Chop the flesh and purée in a food processor or blender with the lemon juice and mint until smooth and creamy.

◇ Transfer to a small bowl and stir in the cheese and pepper and season to taste.

◇ Cover with plastic wrap and then top with foil or a tight-fitting lid and chill until required.

◇ Serve the dip with a selection of crudités.

LEFT *Chilled melon and mint soup*
RIGHT *Summer avocado dip with crudités*

SMOKED SALMON 'SAUSAGES'

~

A mixture of salmon, shrimp and curd cheese is rolled up in rectangles of smoked salmon to form sausage-shaped parcels.

8 OUNCES SMOKED SALMON

FILLING

4 OUNCES PEELED SHRIMP

¼ CUP RICOTTA CHEESE

3 SCALLIONS, TRIMMED

1 SMALL CLOVE GARLIC, CRUSHED

GRATED RIND OF 1 LIME

PINCH OF GRATED NUTMEG

SALT AND PEPPER

◇ Carefully remove the waxed paper from between the layers of salmon and cut the strips into 6 rectangles, 3×4 inches, overlapping them if necessary.
◇ Finely chop the smoked salmon trimmings.
◇ Place all the remaining ingredients in a food processor and purée until smooth. Transfer to a bowl and stir in the chopped salmon.
◇ Place ⅙th of the mixture along 1 narrow edge of each smoked salmon rectangle, and roll up to form a sausage shape. Wrap up each sausage individually in plastic wrap and twist the ends to seal the filling.
◇ Chill until required, transport in a cooler and serve sliced, with crusty bread, crisp crackers or a salad.

ICED CUCUMBER SOUP

~

For the best result serve this soup thoroughly chilled, preferably adding a few ice cubes at the last minute.

3 LARGE CUCUMBERS

9 SCALLIONS, TRIMMED AND CHOPPED

1 TABLESPOON CHOPPED FRESH DILL

2 CARTONS ALFALFA SPROUTS

JUICE OF 1 LEMON

2 TABLESPOONS OLIVE OIL

1¼ CUPS YOGURT

⅔ CUP LIGHT CREAM

TO SERVE

ICE CUBES (OPTIONAL)

MUSTARD AND CRESS

◇ Peel and de-seed the cucumbers and cut them into thick slices.
◇ Place in a food processor or blender, with all the remaining ingredients and blend until smooth.
◇ Chill thoroughly in the refrigerator and transfer to a thermos just before required.
◇ Add a couple of ice cubes and alfalfa sprouts to each serving, if wished.

TOP LEFT *Smoked salmon 'sausages'*
BOTTOM RIGHT *Iced cucumber soup*

CURRIED EGGS

~

This is a delicious and attractive way to serve hard-cooked eggs. A curried mayonnaise sauce is poured over halved eggs, and sprinkled with a little sieved egg yolk. The eggs, sauce and garnish should be transported separately, and put together just before serving.

3 TABLESPOONS OLIVE OIL

1 SMALL ONION, CHOPPED

1 CLOVE GARLIC, CHOPPED

1 TEASPOON GRATED FRESH ROOT GINGER

1 TABLESPOON CURRY POWDER

¾ CUP READY-MADE MAYONNAISE

5 TABLESPOONS YOGURT

1 TABLESPOON LEMON JUICE

1 TABLESPOON CHOPPED FRESH CILANTRO OR PARSLEY

4 SCALLIONS, TRIMMED AND CHOPPED

12 HARD-COOKED EGGS, PEELED

SALT AND PEPPER

TO GARNISH

CILANTRO SPRIGS (OPTIONAL)

◇ Heat the oil and sauté the onion, garlic, ginger and curry powder for 5 minutes. Pour the oil through a fine strainer into a bowl and cool slightly.

◇ Stir all the remaining ingredients except for the eggs into the cooled oil and season to taste.

◇ Cut 9 of the eggs in half and arrange, cut side down, on a large deep-lipped plate, or shallow dish. Cover with plastic wrap and chill.

◇ Finely chop the remaining eggs, except the yolk of one, and stir into the mayonnaise mixture. Place in a dish with a tight-fitting lid, and chill until ready to transport.

◇ Sieve the remaining yolk, transfer to a screw-top jar, and chill. Transport all separately in a cooler.

◇ Spoon the sauce over the eggs and garnish with the sieved yolk and cilantro sprigs. Serve with wholewheat bread.

EGGPLANT PÂTÉ

~

This makes a delicious vegetarian spread or dip.

1 LARGE EGGPLANT

1 SMALL CLOVE GARLIC, CRUSHED

1 TABLESPOON CHOPPED FRESH CILANTRO OR
1 TEASPOON GROUND CORIANDER SEEDS

1 TABLESPOON LEMON JUICE

2 TEASPOONS TAHINI PASTE

¼ TEASPOON GROUND CUMIN

1 TABLESPOON OLIVE OIL

SALT AND PEPPER

◇ Heat the oven to 400°F. Prick the eggplant all over with the point of a sharp knife and bake for 30 minutes, until the skin is wrinkled and the flesh feels soft. Remove from the oven and leave to cool for 10 minutes.

◇ Peel and discard the skin and chop the flesh.

◇ Place in a food processor or blender with all the remaining ingredients and blend until smooth.

◇ Transfer to a small dish, cover and chill until required.

◇ Serve the pâté with pita bread or a selection of vegetable crudités.

BOTTOM *Curried eggs*
TOP *Eggplant pâté*

BACON & MUSHROOM PIE

~

The availability of ready-made piecrust mix enables you to make this pie without having to take the extra time of making your own pastry. However, if you do choose to make it yourself, line the pan with pastry and continue as the recipe directs.

1 STICK PIECRUST MIX

1 TABLESPOON OLIVE OIL

1½ CUPS CHOPPED BACON

1 CUP SLICED MUSHROOMS

2 TEASPOONS CHOPPED FRESH SAGE

2 EGGS

¾ CUP LIGHT CREAM

PINCH OF GROUND MACE

⅓ CUP GRATED GRUYÈRE OR CHEDDAR CHEESE

SALT AND PEPPER

◇ Roll out the pastry thinly, and use to line an 8-inch flan pan. Chill the pastry while preparing the filling. Heat the oven to 450°F and place a baking sheet on the center rack.
◇ Heat the oil and stir-fry the bacon, over a high heat, until golden. Remove with a slotted spoon and drain.
◇ Add the mushrooms and sage to the skillet and stir-fry until just wilted. Drain and cool slightly.
◇ Beat the eggs, cream and seasonings together.
◇ Sprinkle the bacon and mushrooms over the pastry shell, pour in the egg mixture and finally top with the grated cheese.
◇ Place in the oven, on the baking sheet, and bake for 5 minutes. Lower the temperature to 375°F and bake for a further 20-25 minutes until set. Remove from the oven and cool slightly. Chill.
◇ Cover with foil and transport pie in a cooler.

COS SALAD WITH BLUE BRIE DRESSING

~

A crisp green salad that is complemented perfectly by this rich, creamy blue cheese dressing.

DRESSING

3 OUNCES BLUE BRIE

4 TABLESPOONS OLIVE OIL

3 TABLESPOONS YOGURT OR FROMAGE FRAIS

4 TEASPOONS RASPBERRY OR RED WINE VINEGAR

SALT AND PEPPER

SALAD

2 COS OR ICEBERG LETTUCES

4 OUNCES SEEDLESS GREEN GRAPES

1 CUP YOUNG SPINACH LEAVES OR WATERCRESS

2 YOUNG LEEKS, TRIMMED

1 TABLESPOON CHOPPED FRESH CHIVES

½ CUP PUMPKIN SEEDS, TOASTED

◇ Make the dressing: blend the brie, oil and yogurt or fromage frais, in a blender until smooth and stir in the vinegar and seasonings. Pour into a screw-top jar. Chill.
◇ Make the salad: wash the lettuce, pat dry and discard the tough outer leaves. Tear into bite-size pieces and place in a large bowl. Halve the grapes, wash and dry the spinach. Finely slice the leeks and add to the lettuce with the chives. Transfer to a container. Chill.
◇ Transport the dressing, salad and pumpkin seeds separately and toss together just before serving.

BOTTOM *Bacon and mushroom flan*
TOP *Cos salad with blue brie dressing*

SPINACH TORTILLA

~

A Spanish-style omelet, made with spinach and cottage cheese for a fresh and tasty summer dish. Quick and easy to make, tortillas are great picnic food.

1 TABLESPOON OLIVE OIL

1 SMALL ONION, CHOPPED

1 MEDIUM POTATO, PEELED AND DICED

½ TEASPOON GROUND TURMERIC

2 CUPS SHREDDED SPINACH LEAVES

¾ CUP COTTAGE CHEESE

6 EGGS, LIGHTLY BEATEN

PINCH OF GRATED NUTMEG

SALT AND PEPPER

◇ Heat the oil in an 8-inch non-stick skillet and sauté the onion, potato and turmeric over medium heat for 10 minutes, until lightly browned.
◇ Stir in the spinach leaves until they start to wilt.
◇ Beat the cheese and eggs together and pour into the skillet. Cook for 15 minutes, until the tortilla is almost set, then place under a hot broiler to finish off the top.
◇ Remove from the heat and cool in the skillet.
◇ Turn out onto a plate, cover with foil and chill until required.

CARROT & ZUCCHINI SALAD

~

A refreshingly tangy salad which improves with time as the flavors are allowed to mingle.

4 MEDIUM CARROTS, PEELED

4 MEDIUM ZUCCHINI

1 SMALL RED ONION

1 CLOVE GARLIC

1 TEASPOON CHOPPED FRESH TARRAGON

3 TABLESPOONS EXTRA VIRGIN OLIVE OIL

1 TABLESPOON RASPBERRY OR RED WINE VINEGAR

¼ CUP PINENUTS, TOASTED

SALT AND PEPPER

◇ Thinly slice the carrots, zucchini, onion and garlic and place in a large bowl. Add the tarragon and plenty of salt and pepper.
◇ Blend the oil and vinegar together and add to the bowl. Toss salad till well coated and place in a container. Chill.
◇ Transport the nuts in a separate container and sprinkle over the salad just before serving.

LEFT *Spinach tortilla*
RIGHT *Carrot and zucchini salad*

CHICKEN LIVER PÂTÉ

~

Serve the pâté with French bread, and try it with a spoonful of red currant jelly for a tasty alternative. Set a few herb leaves into the butter if wished: the melted butter will need about 1 hour to set, so if time is short, leave this part out.

8 OUNCES CHICKEN LIVERS

⅔ CUP UNSALTED BUTTER

1 CLOVE GARLIC, CRUSHED

1 TEASPOON CHOPPED FRESH THYME

2 TABLESPOONS PORT OR BRANDY

TO GARNISH

A FEW PRETTY HERB LEAVES

TO SERVE

FRENCH BREAD

RED CURRANT JELLY (OPTIONAL)

◇ Wash and dry the chicken livers and discard any membrane or discolored bits.

◇ Heat 2 tablespoons butter and stir-fry the livers over a high heat until browned on the outside but still pink in the center. Remove with a slotted spoon and place in a food processor or blender.

◇ Sauté the garlic and thyme for 1 minute, add the port or brandy and scrape the bottom of the pan with a wooden spatula.

◇ Add to the chicken livers, with ⅓ cup of remaining butter. Purée until smooth and transfer to a dish.

◇ If you have time, gently melt the remaining butter and pour through a fine sieve, over the pâté. Set a few herb leaves in the butter and chill until set.

◇ Cover with foil or a tight-fitting lid and transport in a cooler.

◇ Serve the pâté with the bread and a spoonful of red currant jelly, if wished.

SAUSAGE, BACON & APRICOT KABOBS

~

Serve these tangy glazed kabobs as an appetizer.

KABOBS

12 SLICES BACON

12 COCKTAIL SAUSAGES

3 LARGE FIRM APRICOTS, PITTED AND QUARTERED

GLAZE

2 TABLESPOONS APRICOT PRESERVES

2 TEASPOONS DIJON MUSTARD

1 TEASPOON WORCESTERSHIRE SAUCE

1 TEASPOON LEMON JUICE

6 BAMBOO SKEWERS

◇ Roll up the bacon into rolls and thread onto the skewers, alternating them with the sausages and apricot quarters.

◇ Mix all the glaze ingredients together and brush over the kabobs.

◇ Place under a preheated broiler and cook for 8-10 minutes on each side, brushing frequently with the glaze, until crisp and golden.

◇ Wrap in foil and chill.

FRONT *Chicken liver pâté*
BACK *Sausage, bacon and apricot kabobs*

PASTA SALAD WITH TUNA SAUCE

~

The pasta is mixed with this tangy dressing while still hot, so it will absorb more flavor as it cools.

====

12 OUNCES TRI-COLOR PASTA

DRESSING

⅔ CUP EXTRA VIRGIN OLIVE OIL

2 TABLESPOONS WHITE WINE VINEGAR

2 TABLESPOONS TOMATO KETCHUP

1 TEASPOON PAPRIKA

¼ TEASPOON CAYENNE PEPPER

SALAD

7-OUNCE CAN TUNA, DRAINED

1 BUNCH SCALLIONS

2 TABLESPOONS CHOPPED FRESH DILL

====

◇ Cook the pasta in boiling salted water for 10-12 minutes, until 'al dente' (just done). Drain and place in a large bowl.
◇ Blend the dressing ingredients together until combined and toss with the pasta.
◇ Stir in the tuna, onions and dill and place in a container. Chill thoroughly.

WATERCRESS & SALMON ROLLS

~

Watercress, canned salmon and ready-made mayonnaise combine to make a tasty filling for fresh bread rolls.

====

1 BUNCH WATERCRESS

1 TABLESPOON CHOPPED FRESH TARRAGON

⅔ CUP READY-MADE MAYONNAISE

GRATED RIND AND JUICE OF 1 LEMON

2 7-OUNCE CANS PINK SALMON, DRAINED

PINCH OF GRATED NUTMEG

SALT AND PEPPER

TO SERVE

6 LARGE BREAD ROLLS

WATERCRESS (OPTIONAL)

====

◇ Wash and dry the watercress, discarding any large stalks. Chop finely and blend with the tarragon, mayonnaise, lemon rind and juice.
◇ Flake the salmon and stir into the mayonnaise with nutmeg, salt and pepper.
◇ Cut the rolls in half and fill with the salmon mixture and extra fresh watercress, if wished. Wrap in waxed paper or foil and chill thoroughly.

BACK *Pasta salad with tuna sauce*
FRONT *Watercress and salmon rolls*

SALADE NIÇOISE

~

This is one of many variations of a classic Salade Niçoise. I particularly like the addition of canned artichoke hearts, but 3 chopped hard-cooked eggs can be substituted instead.

==

SALAD

2 2-OUNCE CANS ANCHOVIES, DRAINED

A LITTLE MILK

4 OUNCES GREEN BEANS, TRIMMED

1 14-OUNCE CAN ARTICHOKE HEARTS, DRAINED

½ CUP PITTED BLACK OLIVES

1 TABLESPOON CHOPPED FRESH CHIVES

1 TABLESPOON CHOPPED FRESH BASIL

6 LARGE TOMATOES, QUARTERED

DRESSING

4 TABLESPOONS VIRGIN OLIVE OIL

1 TABLESPOON BALSAMIC OR RED WINE VINEGAR

2 TEASPOONS WHOLEGRAIN MUSTARD

PINCH OF SUGAR

SALT AND PEPPER

TO GARNISH

BASIL LEAVES

==

◇ Soak the drained anchovies in a little milk for 10 minutes, drain, wash under cold water and pat dry.
◇ Blanch the trimmed green beans in boiling salted water for 2 minutes. Drain beans, rinse under cold water and pat dry.
◇ Quarter the artichoke hearts or peel and chop the eggs (if using) and place in a large bowl. Add the anchovies, beans, olives, herbs and tomatoes and mix well.
◇ Blend all the dressing ingredients together and pour over the salad. Cover and chill until required.
◇ Stir the salad and dressing well, garnish with basil leaves and serve with crisp fresh bread.

LEEKS À LA GRECQUE

~

My variation of the classic chilled and marinated vegetable dish. Use tender young leeks for the best results, as they are sweet and need little cooking to become tender.

==

12 SMALL YOUNG LEEKS, TRIMMED

MARINADE

1¼ CUPS DRY WHITE WINE

⅔ CUP VEGETABLE STOCK

1 TABLESPOON WHITE WINE VINEGAR

2 SPRIGS THYME

1 TEASPOON FENNEL SEEDS, CRUSHED

1 TEASPOON CORIANDER SEEDS, CRUSHED

½ TEASPOON WHITE PEPPERCORNS

4 LARGE TOMATOES, PEELED, SEEDED AND CHOPPED

PINCH OF SUGAR

SALT AND PEPPER

TO SERVE

⅓ CUP PITTED BLACK OLIVES, CHOPPED

==

◇ Wash the leeks well and pat dry.
◇ Place in a large skillet and add the wine, stock, vinegar, herb and spices. Bring to a boil, cover and simmer gently for 8-10 minutes, until the leeks are just tender. Test them with the point of a sharp knife.
◇ Remove the leeks with a slotted spoon and transfer to a shallow dish to cool.
◇ Add the remaining marinade ingredients to the skillet and boil for 5 minutes. Cool slightly and pour the mixture over the leeks.
◇ Cover and chill until required and serve topped with chopped black olives.

BOTTOM *Salade Niçoise*
TOP *Leeks à la Grecque*

SICILIAN POTATO SALAD

~

The ingredients in this tasty potato salad are typical of many classic Sicilian dishes.

═══

1 2-OUNCE CAN ANCHOVIES IN OIL, DRAINED

A LITTLE MILK

2 POUNDS NEW POTATOES, SCRUBBED

1 TABLESPOON CAPERS, CHOPPED

1 TABLESPOON CHOPPED FRESH PARSLEY

1 TEASPOON GRATED LEMON RIND

1 TABLESPOON LEMON JUICE

1 SMALL CLOVE GARLIC, CRUSHED

3 TABLESPOONS OLIVE OIL

PEPPER

═══

◇ Place the anchovies in a shallow dish, cover with milk and leave to soak for 10 minutes. Drain the anchovies, wash under cold water and pat dry.

◇ Cut the potatoes into bite-size chunks and cook in boiling salted water for 10-12 minutes, until just cooked.

◇ Meanwhile, chop the anchovies and mash with all the remaining ingredients except the oil. Stir in the oil.

◇ Drain the cooked potatoes and place in a large bowl. Immediately add the anchovy mixture and mix the ingredients together well.

◇ Transfer salad to a plastic container, cover and chill until ready to serve.

THREE BEAN SALAD

~

A combination of fresh and canned beans, fruit and olives is tossed in a mustard dressing.

═══

SALAD

6 OUNCES GREEN BEANS, TRIMMED

¾ CUP CANNED RED KIDNEY BEANS, DRAINED

¾ CUP CANNED WHITE KIDNEY BEANS, DRAINED

¾ CUP CANNED CHICKPEAS, DRAINED

1 RED SWEET PEPPER, SEEDED AND SLICED

½ CUP RAISINS

⅓ CUP PITTED GREEN OLIVES, CHOPPED

2 TABLESPOONS SHREDDED FRESH BASIL LEAVES

DRESSING

4 TABLESPOONS EXTRA VIRGIN OLIVE OIL

1 TABLESPOON RED WINE VINEGAR

2 TEASPOONS DIJON MUSTARD

1 SMALL CLOVE GARLIC, CRUSHED

½ TEASPOON GROUND CUMIN

SALT AND PEPPER

═══

◇ Blanch the trimmed green beans in boiling water for 2 minutes. Drain, rinse under cold water, and pat dry. Place in a large bowl and stir in the remaining salad ingredients.

◇ Blend the dressing ingredients together and pour over the salad, toss well and transfer to a plastic container.

◇ Cover and chill until ready to serve.

BACK *Sicilian potato salad*
FRONT *Three bean salad*

STRAWBERRY CHEESE
WITH SHORTBREAD

~

A sweet/savory cheese which is simply strawberries and cream cheese, served with melt-in-the-mouth shortbread cookies.

═══

SHORTBREAD

1¼ CUPS ALL-PURPOSE FLOUR

½ CUP UNSALTED BUTTER, DICED

¼ CUP SUPERFINE SUGAR

½ TEASPOON GROUND CINNAMON

CHEESE

6 OUNCES STRAWBERRIES, HULLED

SCANT 1 CUP CREAM CHEESE

PEPPER

═══

◇ Make the shortbread: sift the flour into a bowl and cut in the butter until the mixture resembles fine bread-crumbs. Stir in the sugar and spice and work the mixture together to form a firm paste.

◇ Divide in half and roll each piece out to an 8-inch round. Cut each round into 6 triangles and place on a large greased baking sheet.

◇ Bake in a preheated oven at 375°F for 15 minutes, until golden. Remove from the oven and cool on a wire rack.

◇ Meanwhile, prepare the cheese: finely chop the straw-berries and drain on paper towels. Carefully mix with the cheese and pepper and transfer to a small dish with a tight-fitting lid. Chill until required.

◇ Transport the dish in a cooler and serve with the short-bread cookies.

SUMMER BERRY FOOL

~

Fruit fools are wonderfully fresh and fragrant with a high proportion of fruit purée to cream. The mixture for this fool should be just thick, almost holding its shape. Use your favorite summer berry for this recipe – I prefer loganberries, but raspberries, blackberries or strawberries would work equally well.

═══

1½ POUNDS LOGANBERRIES OR OTHER BERRIES

½-¾ CUP CONFECTIONERS' SUGAR

3 TABLESPOONS PORT

1 CUP HEAVY CREAM

TO SERVE

COOKIES, (BRANDY SNAPS, ROLLED WAFERS OR
SHORTBREAD)

═══

◇ Purée the fruit in a food processor or blender and pass through a fine sieve to remove the seeds. Transfer to a mixing bowl.

◇ Sift in the sugar, beat well until combined and stir in the port.

◇ Lightly whip the cream and gradually beat in the fruit mixture until just thick.

◇ Transfer to a plastic container with a tight-fitting lid and chill until required.

◇ Transport the fool in its container, or in a thermos, in a cooler and serve in individual glasses or bowls with the cookies of your choice.

TOP LEFT *Strawberry cheese with shortbread*
BOTTOM RIGHT *Summer berry fool*

RICOTTA, NUT & HONEY CHEESE

~

This recipe is based on a classic Spanish sweet, made here with ricotta cheese. It is delightful.

1½ CUPS RICOTTA CHEESE

½ CUP PINENUTS, TOASTED

4 TEASPOONS HONEY

½ TEASPOON GROUND CINNAMON

¼ TEASPOON FRESHLY GRATED NUTMEG

TO SERVE

SELECTION OF FRESH FRUIT (FIGS, DATES,
NECTARINES, PEARS, APPLES, STRAWBERRIES)

◇ Place the cheese in a bowl. Chop the pinenuts and stir into the ricotta with the remaining ingredients.

◇ Line a strainer with a large piece of cheesecloth and spoon in the cheese mixture. Pull over the ends of the cheesecloth and set the strainer over a bowl. Place a heavy weight on top and drain for 30 minutes.

◇ Remove the weight and transfer the mixture, in the cheesecloth, to a plastic container. Chill until required.

◇ Transport in a cooler and serve straight from the cheesecloth, with a selection of your favorite fruits.

REFRIGERATOR CAKE

~

This is a no-cook chocolate and gingersnap cake which needs to be chilled for about 1 hour in order to firm up, before transporting to the picnic. Make it the first dish you prepare and your thinking ahead will be well rewarded.

2¼ CUPS COARSELY CRUSHED GINGER SNAPS

⅔ CUP FINELY CHOPPED DRIED FIGS

3 TABLESPOONS COCOA POWDER

1 TABLESPOON CHOPPED CANDIED GINGER

⅓ CUP UNSALTED BUTTER

3 SQUARES UNSWEETENED CHOCOLATE

2 TABLESPOONS HONEY

◇ Place waxed paper on the bottom of a 7-inch spring-form pan with a removable bottom.

◇ Combine the ginger snaps, figs, 2 tablespoons cocoa powder and candied ginger in a bowl.

◇ Melt the butter, chocolate and honey together in a small pan and pour into the bowl. Stir well until the ginger snaps are coated and spoon into the prepared pan. Press into the sides and smooth the surface.

◇ Chill at least 1 hour until firm. Sift over the final 1 tablespoon cocoa powder, cover the pan with foil and transport in a cooler. Serve cut into wedges.

CENTRE *Ricotta, nut and honey cheese*
RIGHT *Refrigerator cake*

SPARKLING FRUIT CUP

~

The mixed fruit is soaked in the port and brandy and served with chilled sparkling wine.

¼ CUP PORT

¼ CUP BRANDY

2 NECTARINES OR PEACHES, PITTED AND SLICED

12 STRAWBERRIES, HULLED AND HALVED

12 RASPBERRIES

1 BOTTLE CHILLED SPARKLING WINE

◇ Combine the port, brandy and fruit together and place in a plastic container, with a tight-fitting lid.
◇ Chill until required and pour in the chilled wine just before serving.

ORCHARD BLOOM

~

A purée of pears and cinnamon, teamed with sparkling apple juice, makes a wonderful thirst-quenching summer drink.

PURÉE

3 LARGE RIPE PEARS, PEELED, CORED AND CHOPPED

1 TEASPOON GROUND CINNAMON

1 TEASPOON LEMON JUICE

1 TEASPOON SUGAR

TO SERVE

1 BOTTLE CHILLED SPARKLING APPLE JUICE

CRUSHED ICE

◇ Place the pears, cinnamon, lemon juice and sugar in a small pan and simmer, covered, over a very low heat for 12-15 minutes, until the pears are tender.
◇ Cool slightly and purée until smooth. Cool and spoon into a screw-top jar. Chill.
◇ Divide the purée between 6 medium glasses and pour in the apple juice. Add the crushed ice and serve.

PINK PERIL

~

Aptly named for its vibrant color and deceptive kick! The measures in this recipe are given for a single serving. Use ruby grapefruit if available.

CHILLED VODKA

CRUSHED ICE

¼ CUP FRESHLY SQUEEZED GRAPEFRUIT JUICE

¼ CUP CRANBERRY JUICE

TO DECORATE

MARASCHINO CHERRIES

◇ Pour a measure of vodka into a small cocktail glass and add a little crushed ice.
◇ Top up with the grapefruit and cranberry juices and decorate the glass with a maraschino cherry.
◇ Serve at once.

CENTRE *Sparkling fruit cup*
LEFT *Orchard bloom*
RIGHT *Pink peril*

FOOD WITH FIRE

Grilling outdoors is an especially rewarding experience, as the aromas of grilling food and fresh air surround you; even the simplest dish seems to taste better when barbecued.

This chapter contains recipes intended for just such a culinary experience, with some delectable alternatives to everyday grilling. You'll also find recipes for mouth-watering appetizers and make-ahead desserts.

Barbecue equipment comes in a multitude of types, from small and portable to the gas or electric grills — there are even disposable grills made of aluminum foil.

You may also 'construct' a grill, using a few bricks and a metal tray to hold coals. A hole dug in the sand will also suffice quite well. A wire grill or even a spare oven rack can then be used to support the food over the homemade barbecue.

While wood may be used for fuel (some swear by it!), the most popular form is the charcoal briquette, whose dense hardwood and low resin content give a more intense, uniform heat. Especially tantalizing flavors may be produced with hickory or mesquite flavored charcoal. Charcoal lighter fluid is a great aid in starting the fire and comes in liquid or gel forms.

When the flames have died down, usually after 35-45 minutes, coals should take on a glowing, ashen quality, which indicates they are ready to cook over. Place food on a lightly oiled grill or grid, an inch or two above the coals, being careful to avoid scorching from flames that are still too hot.

Safety is largely a matter of common sense: avoid a confined space when setting up the barbecue, keeping away from the house and out from under trees; use only lighter fluids specifically for use with barbecues, never gasoline; use long-handled tongs and other tools to avoid burns; allow a transportable grill to cool completely before picking up to bring home.

CONTENTS

Lentil and cashew nut soup
Moroccan spiced garlic bread..36

Shrimp and monkfish kabobs with coconut salsa
Persian chicken kabobs..38

Red mullet with fennel
Tomato and olive oil bruschetta..40

Glazed lamb steaks
Southern chicken wings with spicy barbecue sauce.............42

Beef and vegetable kabobs with herby yogurt sauce.............44

Chinese spiced riblets
Bacon and banana kabobs...46

Broiled peppers
Sesame zucchini..48

Tuna fish saté
Pan-fried fish steaks..50

Baked sweet potatoes with garlic and thyme
Foil-baked mushrooms...52

Fruit kabobs with honey glaze
Foiled rum bananas...54

Apricot and pistachio pie
Peach and cinnamon puffs..56

Sangria
Blushing strawberry fizz
Homemade lemonade...58

LENTIL & CASHEW NUT SOUP

~

A creamy heart-warming soup, ideal for a fall evening barbecue.

2 TABLESPOONS OLIVE OIL

1 LARGE ONION, CHOPPED

1 CLOVE GARLIC, CRUSHED

1½ CUPS CHOPPED CARROTS

2 TEASPOONS GROUND CORIANDER

1 TEASPOON GROUND CUMIN

½ TEASPOON GROUND TURMERIC

½ TEASPOON GROUND CINNAMON

⅔ CUP LENTILS, WASHED

4¼ CUPS CHICKEN OR VEGETABLE STOCK

1 BAYLEAF

1½ CUPS CASHEW NUTS, TOASTED

JUICE OF 1 LEMON

SALT AND PEPPER

◇ Heat the oil in a large saucepan and fry the onion and garlic for 5 minutes, until lightly browned. Add the carrots and spices and stir-fry for 2-3 minutes, until the vegetables are well coated.
◇ Add the lentils, stock and bayleaf, bring to a boil, cover and simmer gently for 20 minutes, until the lentils and carrots are soft.
◇ Remove the bayleaf and purée the soup in a food processor or blender until smooth and return to the pan.
◇ Grind the nuts and lemon juice to a coarse paste in a blender or food processor, stir into the soup, heat through and season to taste. Alternatively, transport the nuts in a separate container and add to the soup before serving.
◇ Transfer the soup to a thermos to keep hot.

MOROCCAN SPICED GARLIC BREAD

~

Add a little spice to your life with this Moroccan version of garlic bread. This recipe will serve 6 or 12 people depending on how hungry they are.

2 SMALL FRENCH BREAD LOAVES

¾ CUP BUTTER, SOFTENED

2 CLOVES GARLIC, CRUSHED

1 TABLESPOON TOMATO PASTE

1 TABLESPOON CHOPPED FRESH CILANTRO

1 TABLESPOON CHOPPED FRESH PARSLEY

½ TEASPOON GROUND CUMIN

½ TEASPOON GROUND PAPRIKA

PINCH OF CAYENNE PEPPER

SALT

◇ Cut the bread into ½-inch slices, without cutting all the way through to the bottom.
◇ Cream all the remaining ingredients together and spread a little spiced butter between bread slices. Spread any remaining butter all over the bread.
◇ Wrap the bread loaves in foil and turn the edges over to seal.
◇ Bake the bread in a preheated oven at 400°F for 10 minutes, open the foil and bake for a further 5 minutes. Alternatively, place the foil parcels over the coolest part of a hot barbecue and cook for 5 minutes, turn over and cook for a further 5 minutes.
◇ Serve piping hot.

FRONT *Lentil and cashew nut soup*
BACK *Moroccan spiced garlic bread*

SHRIMP & MONKFISH KABOBS WITH COCONUT SALSA

~

The tantalizing aroma of these kabobs cooking on the barbecue is certain to get your taste buds going. The kabobs are quick to cook and, served with this unusual coconut salsa, are quite delicious.

SALSA

¾-1 CUP OLIVE OIL

2 TEASPOONS SESAME OIL

8 SCALLIONS, TRIMMED AND FINELY CHOPPED

2 TABLESPOONS CHOPPED FRESH CILANTRO

RIND AND JUICE OF 2 LIMES

1-2 DRIED RED CHILLIES, CRUSHED

⅔ CUP COCONUT

KABOBS

18 RAW LARGE SHRIMP

1 POUND MONKFISH FILLETS

4 LIMES, SLICED

6 METAL SKEWERS

SESAME OIL FOR BASTING

◇ Make the salsa: heat both oils together in a small pan and sauté the scallions and cilantro for 2 minutes. Remove from the heat and stir in the remaining ingredients. Transfer to a small dish and leave to cool.
◇ Wash and dry the shrimp and, if desired, remove the heads and shells. Cut the monkfish into 1-inch pieces.
◇ Thread the shrimp, monkfish and lime slices alternately onto the metal skewers, brush all over with sesame oil and place on the barbecue. Cook the kabobs over medium-hot coals for 6-8 minutes turning and basting with oil, from time to time, until the shrimp and monkfish are lightly browned and cooked through.
◇ Serve at once with the coconut salsa.

PERSIAN CHICKEN KABOBS

~

A unique blend of nuts, spices and yogurt make these chicken kabobs an unusual and exotic dish. Use 2 skewers to make each kabob, as the chicken pieces are quite large.

12 CHICKEN THIGHS

MARINADE

¾ CUP YOGURT

1 SMALL ONION, MINCED

2 LARGE CLOVES GARLIC, CRUSHED

¾ CUP CASHEW NUTS, TOASTED AND GROUND

JUICE OF 1 LEMON

1 TEASPOON GROUND CUMIN

1 TEASPOON APPLE PIE SPICE

PINCH OF CAYENNE PEPPER

SALT AND PEPPER

TO SERVE

LEMON WEDGES

12 BAMBOO SKEWERS

◇ Skin the chicken and cut out the bone. Cut each one in half and place in a large bowl.
◇ Blend the marinade ingredients together until combined and pour into the bowl. Stir well until the chicken pieces are well coated. Cover and marinate in the refrigerator for at least 4 hours or overnight.
◇ Soak the skewers in cold water for 30 minutes. Drain chicken pieces. Pat dry and thread the chicken pieces onto each pair of skewers to make 6 large kabobs.
◇ Cook over medium-hot coals for 7-8 minutes on each side, until the chicken is lightly browned all over.
◇ Serve the kabobs hot with lemon wedges.

BACK *Shrimp and monkfish kabobs with coconut salsa*
FRONT *Persian chicken kabobs*

RED MULLET
WITH FENNEL

~

This firm-fleshed fish is ideal to barbecue, and has few little bones to contend with. The aroma of the fennel and red mullet barbecuing together is truly mouthwatering.

6 6-OUNCE RED MULLET, SCALED AND GUTTED

2 SMALL FENNEL BULBS, THICKLY SLICED

MARINADE

¼ CUPS OLIVE OIL

5 TABLESPOONS DRY WHITE WINE

1 CLOVE GARLIC, ROUGHLY CHOPPED

1 SMALL RED CHILLI, SEEDED AND SLICED

4 SPRIGS THYME, BRUISED

2 SPRIGS PARSLEY, BRUISED

1 TEASPOON CORIANDER SEEDS, COARSELY CRUSHED

½ TEASPOON FENNEL SEEDS

SALT AND PEPPER

◇ Wash the mullet inside and out and dry well. Cut 3 small slashes through the skin of the fish on both sides, and place in a large, shallow dish. Add the fennel slices.
◇ Mix the marinade ingredients together and pour over the fish. Cover and marinate for several hours or over-night in the refrigerator, turning the fish occasionally.
◇ Remove the mullet and fennel from the marinade. Grill the fish over medium-hot coals for 4-5 minutes per side and the fennel for 2-3 minutes per side until both are cooked and lightly browned.
◇ Serve immediately with Tomato and Olive Oil Bruschetta and a crisp green salad.

TOMATO & OLIVE
OIL BRUSCHETTA

~

An Italian-style garlic toast, topped with juicy tomatoes, bruschetta can either be broiled conventionally and served while a main dish is being grilled, or the bread can be toasted over the coals and served as an accompanying dish. Both methods are given, and either way it's delicious.

1 SMALL ITALIAN OR FRENCH BREAD LOAF

2 CLOVES GARLIC, HALVED

6 LARGE RIPE TOMATOES, THINLY SLICED

6 LARGE BASIL LEAVES, SHREDDED

ABOUT 5 TABLESPOONS VIRGIN OLIVE OIL

SALT AND PEPPER

◇ To broil: slice the bread in half lengthways and broil on both sides for 1-2 minutes.
◇ Rub the garlic cloves all over the toast, and top with the tomato slices, basil leaves and salt and pepper.
◇ Drizzle liberally with oil and broil for 3-4 minutes, or until the tomatoes are sizzling.
◇ Cut into fingers and serve piping hot.

◇ To barbecue: marinate the tomatoes, basil, oil and sea-sonings together for 30 minutes.
◇ Slice the bread in half lengthways and toast both sides over hot coals until lightly golden. Rub the garlic all over the toast and top with the marinated tomato mixture. Cut into fingers and serve.

BOTTOM *Red mullet with fennel*
TOP *Tomato and olive oil bruschetta*

GLAZED LAMB STEAKS

~

Infused by the flavors of the marinade, these succulent lamb steaks are spread with honey and mustard, which becomes a crisp golden glaze when barbecued.

===

6 LAMB STEAKS

MARINADE

3 CLOVES GARLIC, HALVED

6 SPRIGS MINT, BRUISED

6 SPRIGS ROSEMARY, BRUISED

⅔ CUP OLIVE OIL

SALT AND PEPPER

GLAZE

9 TABLESPOONS WHOLEGRAIN MUSTARD

3 TABLESPOONS CLEAR HONEY

3 TABLESPOONS CHOPPED FRESH MINT

===

◇ Wash and dry the steaks and rub all over with the garlic, salt and pepper. Lay half the mint and rosemary sprigs in the base of a large shallow dish. Place the lamb on top and cover with the remaining herbs. Pour the oil over all, cover and marinate in the refrigerator for several hours or overnight.

◇ Remove the steaks from the marinade and pat dry.

◇ Mix the glaze ingredients and spread over lamb.

◇ Cook over medium coals for 6-8 minutes on each side, until the lamb is glazed and cooked through. The meat should still be slightly pink in the middle.

◇ Serve the lamb steaks hot with Foil-Baked Mushrooms (see page 52) and Broiled Peppers (see page 48).

SOUTHERN CHICKEN WINGS WITH SPICY BARBECUE SAUCE

~

This spicy sauce is an old favorite and is highly recommended by all who have tried it.

===

SAUCE

1¼ CUPS TOMATO KETCHUP

6 TABLESPOONS HONEY

4 TABLESPOONS WORCESTERSHIRE SAUCE OR 2 TEASPOONS HOT PEPPER SAUCE

2 TABLESPOONS WHITE WINE VINEGAR

2 TEASPOONS MUSTARD

18 CHICKEN WINGS

===

◇ Blend the sauce ingredients together until smooth.

◇ Brush the chicken wings with a little sauce and place over medium coals. Cook for 15-20 minutes, turning and basting frequently until the glaze is crisp and golden, and the chicken is tender.

◇ Allow to cool slightly before serving with Baked Sweet Potatoes with Garlic and Thyme (see page 52) and a fresh summer salad.

RIGHT *Glazed lamb steaks*
LEFT *Southern chicken wings with spicy barbecue sauce*

BEEF & VEGETABLE KABOBS WITH HERBY YOGURT SAUCE

~

Cubes of beef and mixed vegetables are marinated, threaded onto skewers, barbecued and served with a herby yogurt sauce.

KABOBS

2 POUNDS LEAN BEEF

12 PEARL ONIONS

24 BUTTON MUSHROOMS

2 RED SWEET PEPPERS

2 YELLOW SWEET PEPPERS

4 LARGE ZUCCHINI

MARINADE

⅔ CUP OLIVE OIL

1 TABLESPOON LEMON JUICE

1 TABLESPOON CORIANDER SEEDS, CRUSHED

2 TEASPOONS CUMIN SEEDS, CRUSHED

2 SPRIGS THYME, BRUISED

2 SPRIGS SAGE, BRUISED

1 TEASPOON FRESH GREEN PEPPERCORNS, CRUSHED

PINCH OF FRESHLY GRATED NUTMEG

SAUCE

1¼ CUPS YOGURT

1 TABLESPOON LEMON JUICE

1 TABLESPOON CHOPPED FRESH MINT

1 TABLESPOON CHOPPED FRESH DILL

1 TEASPOON GROUND CUMIN

PINCH OF CAYENNE PEPPER

SALT AND PEPPER

24 BAYLEAVES

12 METAL SKEWERS

◇ Cut the beef into cubes. Prepare the vegetables: peel and halve the onions, wash and dry the mushrooms, de-seed the peppers and cut each one into 12 pieces. Wash and dry the zucchini and cut into 6×1-inch slices.

◇ Place the beef and vegetables in a large bowl.

◇ Prepare the marinade: blend the oil and lemon juice together, pour into the bowl and add the remaining marinade ingredients. Toss well together, cover and marinate in the refrigerator for several hours or overnight.

◇ Prepare the yogurt sauce: blend all the ingredients together in a small bowl and set aside.

◇ 30 minutes before assembling the kabobs, soak the bayleaves in cold water. Drain and pat dry.

◇ Thread the beef, vegetables and bayleaves alternately onto the metal skewers and cook over medium-hot coals for 15 minutes. Turning the kabobs and basting with any marinade or extra olive oil once. The beef and vegetables should be browned and tender.

◇ Serve 2 kabobs per person with a generous spoonful of the herby yogurt sauce.

Beef and vegetable kabobs with herby yogurt sauce

CHINESE SPICED RIBLETS

~

Riblets are ribs that have been cut in half to make them easier to handle. Boiling the riblets in water and vinegar tenderizes the meat which is then cooked quickly over a hot barbecue, to become succulent and crispy.

2 POUNDS PORK SPARE RIBLETS

3 TABLESPOONS WINE VINEGAR

3 TABLESPOONS HONEY

3 TABLESPOONS YELLOW BEAN PASTE

1 TABLESPOON SOY SAUCE

1 TABLESPOON DRY SHERRY

2 TEASPOONS SHERRY VINEGAR

1-INCH FRESH ROOT GINGER, PEELED

½ TEASPOON CHINESE FIVE SPICE POWDER

PINCH OF CAYENNE PEPPER

◇ Place the riblets in a large saucepan, add the wine vinegar and enough water to cover. Bring to a boil and simmer gently for 45 minutes, skimming the surface from time to time. Drain and allow to cool.

◇ Blend the honey, yellow bean paste, soy sauce, sherry and sherry vinegar together. Crush the ginger in a garlic press to extract the juice and add to the honey mixture with the spices. Pour over the riblets and marinate in the refrigerator for several hours, turning frequently.

◇ Barbecue the spiced riblets over medium coals, for 5 minutes on each side.

◇ Serve hot.

BACON & BANANA KABOBS

~

Try this combination of sweet and savory and you will be pleasantly surprised at how well they marry together.

36 LARGE SAGE LEAVES

9 SLICES BACON

3 LARGE BANANAS

12 BAMBOO SKEWERS

◇ Soak the skewers in water for 30 minutes. Soak the sage leaves for 10 minutes then pat dry.

◇ Cut the bacon slices in half crossways. Stretch each half to double its length, by running the blunt edge of a knife along it.

◇ Peel and cut each banana into 4 large chunks.

◇ Wrap the stretched bacon around the bananas and thread onto the skewers with a sage leaf dividing each banana chunk. Place over hot coals and cook for 3-4 minutes on each side, until the bacon is crisp and golden.

◇ Serve at once as an appetizer.

BACK *Chinese spiced riblets*
FRONT *Bacon and banana kabobs*

BROILED PEPPERS

~

The smoky flavor the barbecue gives these peppers is exquisite.

═══

6 LARGE SWEET PEPPERS, RED, YELLOW OR ORANGE

DRESSING

4 TABLESPOONS HAZELNUT OR OLIVE OIL

2 TEASPOONS BALSAMIC VINEGAR

1 LARGE CLOVE GARLIC, CHOPPED

2 TABLESPOONS CHOPPED FRESH BASIL

SALT AND PEPPER

═══

◇ Place the peppers over hot coals and cook, turning frequently until the skins blister and become charred.
◇ Put the peppers in a plastic bag and leave to cool and soften for 30 minutes. Peel peppers, discarding the skins and seeds, over a bowl to reserve the juices. Cut peppers into thick slices.
◇ Blend all the dressing ingredients into pepper juices in bowl, except the basil. Pour the dressing over the peppers and sprinkle over the basil.
◇ Serve warm or cold.

SESAME ZUCCHINI

~

A delicious way of cooking zucchini. They are brushed liberally with sesame oil, barbecued and served with a sesame and rosemary dressing.

═══

6 LARGE ZUCCHINI

SESAME OIL TO BRUSH

DRESSING

6 TABLESPOONS SESAME OIL

2 TABLESPOONS LEMON JUICE

1 TABLESPOON CHOPPED FRESH ROSEMARY

PINCH OF SUGAR

SALT AND PEPPER

═══

◇ Cut each zucchini into 4 thick slices and brush with sesame oil. Cook over hot coals for 2-3 minutes on each side, until browned.
◇ Place in a shallow dish, blend the dressing ingredients together and pour over the zucchini.
◇ Serve hot, warm or cold.

TOP *Broiled peppers*
BOTTOM *Sesame zucchini*

TUNA FISH SATÉ

~

Fresh tuna is the perfect fish for this Thai-style saté, as its rich flavor and meaty texture are not overpowered by the soy marinade and peanut sauce.

2 POUNDS FRESH TUNA STEAKS

MARINADE

3 TABLESPOONS LIGHT SOY SAUCE

2 TABLESPOONS WATER

1 TABLESPOON SESAME OIL

1 TABLESPOON HONEY

1 TABLESPOON DRY SHERRY

JUICE OF 1 LIME

1 CLOVE GARLIC, CRUSHED

1 1-INCH PIECE ROOT GINGER, GRATED

SAUCE

4 TABLESPOONS RAW PEANUTS, GROUND

JUICE OF 1 LIME

2 TABLESPOONS WATER

1 TABLESPOON CREAM OF COCONUT

¼ TEASPOON CAYENNE PEPPER

PINCH OF SUGAR

◇ Wash and dry the tuna and cut into ½-inch cubes.
◇ Blend the marinade ingredients together and pour over the fish in a large shallow dish. Cover. Marinate for 1-2 hours in the refrigerator, turning the fish over occasionally.
◇ Drain and reserve the marinade and thread 6 cubes of tuna onto each skewer. Cover and chill.
◇ Make the sauce: put 6 tablespoons of reserved marinade into a small pan and bring to the boil. Stir in the remaining sauce ingredients and simmer over a low heat, until the sauce thickens slightly. Transfer to a small bowl and leave to cool.
◇ Cook the tuna saté over medium-hot coals for 5-6 minutes, turning frequently and basting with the rest of the marinade, until cooked. Serve with peanut sauce.

PAN-FRIED FISH STEAKS

~

I love the Spanish way of cooking fish on a 'plancha' or griddle, over hot coals, and firm-fleshed fish are particularly good cooked this way.

6 6-OUNCE SWORDFISH, HALIBUT OR SALMON STEAKS

MARINADE

⅔ CUP OLIVE OIL

12 BAYLEAVES, BRUISED

3 CARDAMOM PODS, BRUISED

1 TABLESPOON CHOPPED FRESH PARSLEY

1 TABLESPOON GROUND PAPRIKA

6 LEMON SLICES

SAUCE

6 TABLESPOONS OLIVE OIL

JUICE OF 1 LEMON

1 CLOVE GARLIC, CRUSHED

1 TABLESPOON CHOPPED FRESH PARSLEY

PINCH OF CAYENNE PEPPER

SALT

◇ Wash and dry the fish and place in a large shallow dish.
◇ Pour in the oil and add the remaining marinade ingredients. Cover and marinate for 2-3 hours in the refrigerator, turning the fish over from time to time.
◇ Make the sauce: beat the oil and lemon juice together until thickened and add garlic, parsley, cayenne and salt.
◇ Place the griddle on the grill rack over hot coals, brush with oil and allow it to get really hot. Fry the fish on both sides for 4-6 minutes, until golden and done.
◇ Alternatively, place the fish over medium-hot coals on the grill rack and cook for 4-6 minutes on each side.
◇ Serve the fish with plenty of lemon and garlic sauce poured over, and a fresh green salad.

LEFT *Tuna fish saté*
RIGHT *Pan-fried fish steaks*

BAKED SWEET POTATOES WITH GARLIC & THYME

~

Cooking these sweet potatoes in a double layer of foil seals in their delicious flavor. Ordinary potatoes can be cooked in the same way, but may need a little extra time to cook.

═══

1½ POUNDS SWEET POTATOES, PEELED

6 LARGE PIECES FOIL, FOLDED IN HALF

12 CLOVES GARLIC

12 SPRIGS THYME

⅓ CUP BUTTER, SLICED

SALT AND PEPPER

═══

◇ Cut the potatoes into small chunks and divide among the 6 double layers of foil.

◇ To each pile of potatoes add 2 cloves garlic, 2 sprigs thyme, a few pats of butter and plenty of salt and pepper.

◇ Pull the edges of the foil up and fold over to completely seal the fillings.

◇ Place the parcels over medium-hot coals and cook for 20-25 minutes, until the potatoes are tender. Serve straight from the foil.

FOIL-BAKED MUSHROOMS

~

All the flavor and juices from the mushrooms stay sealed within the foil parcels, making a tasty accompaniment to other barbecued food.

═══

18 SMALL MUSHROOMS

6 LARGE PIECES FOIL, FOLDED IN HALF

⅓ CUP BUTTER, SOFTENED

1 CLOVE GARLIC, CRUSHED

1 TABLESPOON CHOPPED FRESH SAGE

GRATED RIND OF 1 LEMON

SALT AND PEPPER

═══

◇ Place 3 mushrooms in the center of each of the 6 double layers of foil.

◇ Cream together the butter, garlic, sage, lemon rind and salt and pepper and spread a spoonful over each mushroom. Pull the edges of the foil up and fold over to seal in the fillings.

◇ Place over medium-hot coals for 6-8 minutes until the mushrooms are tender and juicy.

◇ Serve straight from the foil.

BOTTOM *Baked sweet potatoes with garlic and thyme*
TOP *Foil-baked mushrooms*

FRUIT KABOBS WITH HONEY GLAZE

~

Finish your meal with these succulent, lightly caramelized fruit kabobs.

═══

KABOBS

1 SMALL MANGO, PEELED AND PITTED

½ SMALL PINEAPPLE (CUT LENGTHWAYS), PEELED

2 SMALL APPLES

2 LARGE BANANAS, PEELED

24 KUMQUATS

GLAZE

⅔ CUP HONEY

SHREDDED RIND AND JUICE OF 1 ORANGE

¼ TEASPOON GROUND CLOVES

12 BAMBOO SKEWERS

═══

◇ Cut the mango into 12 chunks. Halve the pineapple, remove the centre core, and cut each piece into 6 slices. Cut the apples into 12 wedges, cut the bananas into 12 thick slices and wash and dry the kumquats.
◇ Thread 2 kumquats and 1 piece each of the other prepared fruits on to each skewer. Place in large shallow dish.
◇ Blend the glaze ingredients together and pour over the kabobs. Cover and marinate for 30 minutes, turning once.
◇ Cook over medium-hot coals for 6-8 minutes, turning and basting frequently with the glaze, until the fruit is browned and sizzling.
◇ Serve hot.

RUM BANANAS

~

Serve these foil-wrapped bananas straight from the barbecue with a spoonful of whipped cream or yogurt.

═══

6 MEDIUM BANANAS, PEELED

6 LARGE PIECES FOIL, FOLDED IN HALF

2 TABLESPOONS CHOPPED CANDIED GINGER

2 TABLESPOONS HONEY

4 TABLESPOONS DARK RUM

2 TABLESPOONS ORANGE JUICE

¼ CUP UNSALTED BUTTER

═══

◇ Cut each banana in half lengthways and place on the center of each of the 6 double layers of foil.
◇ Pull the edges up leaving a small gap at the top and add 1 teaspoon chopped ginger, 1 teaspoon honey, 2 teaspoons rum, 1 teaspoon orange juice and a little of the butter to each package. Fold the edges over to seal well.
◇ Bake over medium-hot coals for 5-6 minutes until the bananas are succulent and tender.
◇ Serve immediately with a little whipped cream or yogurt.

TOP AND LEFT *Fruit kabobs with honey glaze*
BOTTOM RIGHT *Rum bananas*

APRICOT & PISTACHIO PIE

~

This fresh apricot pie tastes as good as it looks, with a layer of apricots arranged over a creamy pistachio custard in a crispy pastry shell.

═══

PASTRY

1¼ CUPS ALL-PURPOSE FLOUR

PINCH OF SALT

½ CUP UNSALTED BUTTER

2 TABLESPOONS SUGAR

1 EGG YOLK

PISTACHIO CUSTARD

1 CUP MILK

3 EGG YOLKS

¼ CUP SUPERFINE SUGAR

5 TABLESPOONS ALL-PURPOSE FLOUR

1 TABLESPOON UNSALTED BUTTER

7 TABLESPOONS GROUND PISTACHIO NUTS

GLAZE

3 TABLESPOONS APRICOT PRESERVES

1 TEASPOON LEMON JUICE

TOPPING

1¼-1½ POUNDS APRICOTS, BLANCHED, PEELED, HALVED AND PITTED

2 TABLESPOONS SHELLED PISTACHIO NUTS

═══

◇ Sift the flour and salt into a bowl and cut in the butter. Stir in the sugar, the egg yolk and 1 tablespoon cold water to form a firm paste. Wrap and chill.
◇ Roll out the dough and line a 9-inch fluted tart pan. Prick the base and chill for 15 minutes.
◇ Bake in a preheated oven at 400°F for 10 to 12 minutes or till golden.
◇ Prepare the custard: heat the milk until just boiling. Whisk the egg yolks and sugar until pale and creamy and beat in the flour. Whisk in the milk and pour through a sieve into a clean pan. Heat gently, stirring, until thickened and cook over a low heat for 2 minutes. Remove from the heat and beat in the butter. Cool slightly, stir in the ground nuts and cover with plastic wrap.
◇ Make the glaze: heat the preserves, 1 teaspoon water and lemon juice, boil for 1 minute, cool.
◇ Spread the custard over the pastry shell and arrange the apricots over the top, pressing down gently. Place a pistachio nut between each gap and spoon over the glaze. Chill till serving time.

PEACH & CINNAMON PUFFS

~

Attractive, individual puff pastry squares, filled with cinnamon and sliced peaches. Serve warm or cold with whipped cream or creme frais.

═══

1½ POUNDS PUFF PASTRY

⅓ CUP UNSALTED BUTTER, SOFTENED

½ CUP GROUND WALNUTS

3 TABLESPOONS SUPERFINE SUGAR

1½ TEASPOONS GROUND CINNAMON

3 PEACHES, PEELED, PITTED AND SLICED

GLAZE

1 EGG BEATEN WITH 1 TABLESPOON MILK

A LITTLE SUGAR

═══

◇ Roll out the pastry thinly and cut into 12 × 5-inch squares. Using a 4½-inch cookie cutter, cut out the middle from 6 of the 12 squares. Chill for 30 minutes.
◇ Cream remaining dry ingredients together and spread in a circle over the 6 uncut pastry squares.
◇ Arrange peach slices over the cinnamon mixture. Wet the edges of the pastry, lay over the cut pastry squares, and press together to seal. With a fork, crimp the edges of the pastry and chill for 15 minutes.
◇ Heat the oven to 425°F. Place puffs on a baking sheet. Brush with the egg glaze and sprinkle a little sugar over the peaches. Bake for 12-15 minutes until golden.

LEFT *Apricot and pistachio pie*
RIGHT *Peach and cinnamon puffs*

SANGRIA

~

There are many variations of this classic Spanish aperitif. I was served this by a friend in Majorca. Substitute brandy for the Grand Marnier, if desired.

1 BOTTLE LIGHT RED WINE

½ CUP FRESHLY SQUEEZED ORANGE JUICE

4 TABLESPOONS GRAND MARNIER

1 ORANGE, THINLY SLICED

1 APPLE, CORED AND THINLY SLICED

1 SMALL LEMON, THINLY SLICED

1¼ CUPS LEMON-LIME CARBONATED BEVERAGE

ICE CUBES

◇ Pour the wine into a large punch bowl or pitcher and stir in the orange juice and Grand Marnier.
◇ Add the fruit and pour in the lemon-lime carbonated beverage, stir well and serve with a handful of ice cubes.

BLUSHING STRAWBERRY FIZZ

~

Crushed fresh strawberries and Cointreau are teamed with champagne to make this summer aperitif.

24 STRAWBERRIES, HULLED

4 TABLESPOONS ORANGE LIQUEUR

1 BOTTLE CHAMPAGNE

◇ Crush the strawberries and blend with the orange liqueur. Divide between 6 glasses and fill glasses with champagne. Serve immediately.

HOMEMADE LEMONADE

~

Make this lemon syrup and keep refrigerated in a screw-top bottle, diluting it with still or sparkling water, as desired.

6 LARGE LEMONS

6 WHOLE CLOVES

5 CUPS BOILING WATER

2 CUPS SUGAR

JUICE OF 2 LEMONS

TO SERVE

1 BOTTLE STILL OR SPARKLING MINERAL WATER

LEMON SLICES

MINT LEAVES

ICE CUBES

◇ Wash and dry the lemons and cut into thick slices. Place in a large bowl with the cloves and pour in the boiling water. Leave to infuse for 24 hours.
◇ Drain and discard the lemon slices and cloves. Place the infused liquid in a large pan, add the sugar and heat gently until dissolved. Bring to a boil and simmer for 10 minutes until the liquid is thick and syrupy. Remove from the heat and cool.
◇ Add the fresh lemon juice and pour into a screw-top bottle, then chill until required.
◇ To serve, put 1-2 tablespoons lemon syrup into each glass, fill glasses with mineral water and decorate with lemon slices and mint leaves if wished, and add ice cubes.

BOTTOM CENTRE *Sangria*
TOP *Blushing strawberry fizz*
BOTTOM LEFT AND RIGHT *Homemade lemonade*

MOVEABLE FEASTS

If you've ever wished to savor a more lavish dinner outdoors, with nature providing a pastoral backdrop, take advantage of the opportunity presented with the sumptuous meals of 'Moveable Feasts'. With these recipes and a little advance notice, it's easy to transform an ordinary get-together into a fantastic picnic.

Relish small details, right down to a quaint picnic basket, bright, crisp linens, and pretty tableware. You might want to add special touches – fresh flowers, or a kerosene lamp or candles for evening. If you like, bring soft music and a portable player.

Whether the occasion is a friendly sports event, family celebration, or a weekend get-away, these evocative dishes will help make the occasion even more memorable.

While not as quick and easy as the recipes found in 'Picnics to Go', the splendid recipes here are well worth the time and effort, with their tendency to elicit smiles, oohs, and ahs from friends and family.

A whole feast can be composed with the following recipes and you will be guaranteed a picnic fit for a king.

CONTENTS

Watercress and herb soup
Potted stilton with port and pear.......................................62

Crab and mango phyllo pastries
Thai-style shrimp eggs 64

Dolmades
Feta, walnut and onion dip...66

Pasta, ham and apricot salad
Minted lamb cutlets 68

Gorgonzola and asparagus quiche
Beet, tarragon and ginger salad.......................................70

Salmon and dill pie
Smoked trout paste..72

Country chicken, ham and herb terrine
Summer greens salad 74

Pissaladière...76

Beef and herb roulade
Onion and pepper relish 78

Pear and cardamom tatin
Caramelized oranges 80

Lemon cheesecake with summer berry sauce
Spiced apple and blueberry muffins....................................82

Peach nectar
Raspberry and ginger cordial
Southern mint julep 84

WATERCRESS & HERB SOUP

~

A fresh, light summer soup. Add the ground almonds if you want a slightly more substantial soup, or if the weather demands a more warming one!

═══

2 TABLESPOONS BUTTER

1 LARGE ONION, CHOPPED

1 CLOVE GARLIC, CRUSHED

4 CUPS WATERCRESS

4 TABLESPOONS CHOPPED FRESH HERBS
(BASIL, CHERVIL, CHIVES, MINT, THYME)

3 CUPS VEGETABLE STOCK

⅔ CUP MILK

⅔ CUP TOASTED AND GROUND ALMONDS
(OPTIONAL)

SALT AND PEPPER

═══

◇ Heat the butter and sauté the onion and garlic for 5 minutes. Stir in the watercress and herbs and pour in the stock and milk.

◇ Bring to a boil, cover and simmer gently for 15 minutes.

◇ Purée the soup in a food processor or blender, until fairly smooth. Heat through, add the almonds if wished, season to taste and pour into a thermos.

POTTED STILTON WITH PORT & PEAR

~

Press the stilton mixture into a pretty dish with a lid, and serve with plenty of fresh celery. This will keep for several days in the refrigerator.

═══

¼ CUP LOW-FAT CREAM CHEESE, SOFTENED

2 TABLESPOONS UNSALTED BUTTER,
SOFTENED

8 OUNCES BLUE STILTON, COARSELY
CRUMBLED

2 TABLESPOONS PORT

1 LARGE FIRM PEAR, PEELED, CORED AND
COARSELY CHOPPED

1 TABLESPOON CHOPPED CELERY LEAVES

PEPPER

TO SERVE

2 BUNCHES CELERY, TRIMMED AND WASHED

═══

◇ Beat together the cream cheese, butter and half the stilton, until smooth and creamy.

◇ Stir in the remaining ingredients and press into a transportable dish. Cover and chill for several hours.

◇ Serve straight from the dish, with the celery.

BACK *Watercress & herb soup*
FRONT *Potted stilton with port & pear*

CRAB & MANGO PHYLLO PASTRIES

~

An exotic combination of crabmeat and mango make a wonderful savory filling for these phyllo pastry packages. If using canned crabmeat, drain well before mixing in.

FILLING

1 TABLESPOON OLIVE OIL

3 SCALLIONS, TRIMMED AND FINELY CHOPPED

1 CLOVE GARLIC, CRUSHED

2 TEASPOONS CHOPPED FRESH CILANTRO

1 CUP FRESH OR CANNED WHITE CRABMEAT

¼ CUP RICOTTA CHEESE

1 SMALL MANGO, PEELED, STONED AND DICED

PINCH OF GROUND MIXED SPICE

PINCH OF CAYENNE PEPPER

SALT AND PEPPER

PASTRY

4 LARGE SHEETS PHYLLO PASTRY

¼ CUP UNSALTED BUTTER, MELTED

◇ Heat the oil and sauté the onion and garlic for 5 minutes. Cool and mix with all the remaining filling ingredients. Season to taste.

◇ Cut the pastry into 12 strips, 3½×14 inches and keep covered with a clean dish towel.

◇ Brush 1 pastry strip with butter and place a heaped tablespoon of filling at one end. Fold over diagonally to form a triangle and continue folding on the diagonal, from side to side to the end of the pastry. Press the ends to seal and brush with butter.

◇ Repeat to make 12 triangular-shaped pastries. Place on a lightly greased baking sheet and bake in a preheated oven at 400°F for 25 minutes, until golden.

◇ Cool on a wire rack and pack carefully in an airtight container. Chill till serving time.

THAI-STYLE SHRIMP EGGS

~

A purée of shrimp and soy sauce is pressed around small hard-cooked eggs, coated with sesame seeds and deep-fried, to make this Thai-style savory snack.

6 SMALL EGGS

1 POUND PEELED SHRIMP

4 SCALLIONS, TRIMMED AND CHOPPED

¾ CUP FRESH WHITE BREADCRUMBS

1 SMALL CLOVE GARLIC, CRUSHED

1 TABLESPOON CHOPPED FRESH CILANTRO

2 TEASPOONS SOY SAUCE

1 TEASPOON GRATED FRESH ROOT GINGER

COATING

A LITTLE ALL-PURPOSE FLOUR

1 EGG, LIGHTLY BEATEN

½-¾ CUP SESAME SEEDS

OIL FOR DEEP FRYING

◇ Boil the eggs for 12 minutes, plunge immediately into cold water and cool before peeling.

◇ Purée the shrimp in a food processor. Add the scallions, breadcrumbs, garlic, cilantro, soy sauce and ginger and purée together until smooth.

◇ Form the mixture into 6 balls, flatten each one out to a 4-inch round. Place a hard-cooked egg in the center of each round, then press the mixture around the egg to completely enclose it. Coat lightly in a little flour, dip into the beaten egg and then into the sesame seeds, until well coated. Chill for 15 minutes.

◇ Heat 4 inches of oil in a heavy-based pan, to a temperature of 350°F. Deep-fry the shrimp eggs in batches, for 2-3 minutes each, until lightly golden. Drain on paper towels; cool and then chill.

FRONT *Crab & mango phyllo pastries*
BACK *Thai-style shrimp eggs*

DOLMADES

~

These savory stuffed grape leaves are a national dish of both Greece and Turkey. The fillings vary slightly, depending on where they are made. This is my particular favorite. Fresh grape leaves can be used, when available. Blanch them in boiling salted water for a few seconds to soften them slightly before use.

═══

25 VINE LEAVES

FILLING

2 TABLESPOONS OLIVE OIL

1 CUP LONG-GRAIN RICE, WASHED

¼ CUP PINE NUTS

3 TABLESPOONS CURRANTS

1 TABLESPOON CHOPPED FRESH MINT

1 TEASPOON SUGAR

1 TEASPOON GROUND CUMIN

¼ TEASPOON GROUND CINNAMON

5 TABLESPOONS WATER

1 TABLESPOON LEMON JUICE

STOCK

JUICE OF 1 LEMON

2 TABLESPOONS OLIVE OIL

WATER

TO SERVE

LEMON WEDGES

YOGURT

═══

◇ Wash the drained grape leaves, pat dry and sort out 18 good-sized leaves. Use the remaining leaves to line an 8-inch square ovenproof dish. Set aside.
◇ Prepare the filling: heat the oil and stir-fry the rice for 1 minute, until transparent. Stir in the remaining ingredients, cover and simmer very gently for 10 minutes. Transfer to a bowl and cool.
◇ Place 2 teaspoons of the rice mixture in the center of a grape leaf. Fold the bottom of the leaf over the filling, then fold in the sides and finally roll up to the top of the leaf, to form a small log-shaped parcel. Repeat to make 18 dolmades. Place in the prepared dish, to fit tightly together.
◇ Put the lemon juice and oil in a 2-cup glass measure and add enough water to equal 1¼ cups. Pour over the dolmades and bake in a preheated oven at 350°F for 1¼ hours, adding extra water if necessary.
◇ Chill till serving time. Serve with lemon wedges and yogurt.

FETA, WALNUT & ONION DIP

~

A tangy, lightly spiced and fruited cheese dip. Serve with pita bread and a selection of vegetable crudités.

═══

7 OUNCES FETA CHEESE, DRAINED

4 TABLESPOONS YOGURT

⅔ CUP CHOPPED WALNUTS

2 TABLESPOONS CHOPPED DRIED FIGS

1 SMALL CLOVE GARLIC, CRUSHED

1 TABLESPOON CHOPPED FRESH DILL

1 TEASPOON GROUND CINNAMON

PINCH OF GROUND NUTMEG

½ RED ONION, CHOPPED

═══

◇ Crumble the feta into a bowl and beat in the yogurt, until combined.
◇ Stir in all the remaining ingredients, cover and chill until required.

BACK LEFT *Dolmades*
FRONT *Feta, walnut & onion dip*

PASTA, HAM & APRICOT SALAD

~

Making your own mayonnaise is surprisingly simple with the use of a food processor or blender. Commercially made mayonnaise can be substituted if you are short of time, in which case, add the strained oil and curry powder to 5 tablespoons of prepared mayonnaise and continue as the recipe directs.

8 OUNCES DRIED PASTA SHAPES

MAYONNAISE

¼ CUP OLIVE OIL

1 SMALL ONION, CHOPPED

2 TEASPOONS CURRY POWDER

OLIVE OIL

1 EGG YOLK

1 TEASPOON LEMON JUICE

SALT AND PEPPER

1 6-OUNCE SLICE FULLY-COOKED HAM

6 OUNCES FRESH APRICOTS

1 SWEET YELLOW PEPPER

¾ CUP CASHEW NUTS, TOASTED

◇ Cook the pasta in boiling salted water, with 1 teaspoon oil, for 10-12 minutes until 'al dente' (just done). Drain, rinse with cold water to prevent further cooking, and cool.
◇ For the mayonnaise: heat the ¼ cup olive oil and sauté the onion and curry powder for 3 minutes. Strain into a glass measuring cup and add enough olive oil to make a scant 1 cup.
◇ Blend the egg yolk, lemon juice, salt and pepper in a food processor or blender, and with the blade running, pour in the oil in a steady stream, through the funnel, until the mixture becomes thick and creamy. If too thick, thin the mayonnaise with boiling water. Cover and set aside.
◇ Cut the ham into short strips. Pit and slice the apri-cots and seed and slice the pepper. Place in a large bowl and toss in the pasta, until combined.
◇ Stir in 4-5 tablespoons mayonnaise and sprinkle with the nuts just before serving.

MINTED LAMB CUTLETS

~

Lamb cutlets are marinated and then broiled, and the marinade is reduced with onion, vinegar and sugar to make a tangy relish.

12 LAMB CUTLETS

MARINADE

½ CUP OLIVE OIL

½ CUP DRY WHITE WINE

4 TABLESPOONS CHOPPED FRESH MINT

RELISH

1 LARGE ONION, VERY FINELY CHOPPED

2 TABLESPOONS WHITE WINE VINEGAR

1 TABLESPOON SUGAR

SALT AND PEPPER

TO GARNISH

MINT LEAVES

◇ Wash the cutlets, pat dry and season with salt and pep-per. Place in a large shallow dish.
◇ Blend the marinade ingredients together and pour over the cutlets. Cover and marinate in the refrigerator for several hours, turning occasionally.
◇ Remove the cutlets from the marinade and place under a hot broiler for 4-5 minutes on each side. Chill.
◇ Meanwhile, make the relish: put the onion, vinegar and sugar into a heavy-based saucepan, add the marinade and simmer over medium heat for 10 minutes. Cool. Pour into a screw-top jar. Chill.

TOP *Pasta, ham & apricot salad*
BOTTOM *Minted lamb cutlets*

GORGONZOLA & ASPARAGUS QUICHE

~

The classic combination of asparagus and blue cheese works particularly well in this savory quiche with the gorgonzola adding a rich creaminess to the filling. (Dolcelatte is a good alternative to gorgonzola.)

PASTRY

1¼ CUPS ALL-PURPOSE FLOUR

3 TABLESPOONS FRESHLY GRATED PARMESAN CHEESE

PINCH OF SALT

½ CUP UNSALTED BUTTER, DICED

1 EGG YOLK

1 TABLESPOON COLD WATER

FILLING

8 OUNCES ASPARAGUS SPEARS

4 OUNCES GORGONZOLA CHEESE, CRUMBLED

1 TABLESPOON CHOPPED FRESH BASIL

SCANT 1 CUP LIGHT CREAM

3 EGGS, LIGHTLY BEATEN

2 TABLESPOONS FRESHLY GRATED PARMESAN CHEESE

SALT AND PEPPER

◇ Make the pastry: combine the flour, cheese and salt in a large bowl, and cut in the butter until the mixture resembles fine breadcrumbs. Work in the egg yolk and water to form a firm paste. Wrap and chill for 20 minutes.
◇ Roll out the dough and use to line a 9-inch fluted pie pan. Prick the base and chill for 15 minutes.
◇ Line pastry with foil and fill with dried beans. Bake in a preheated oven at 400°F for 8 minutes, remove the beans and foil and bake 12-15 minutes more, until the pastry is crisp and lightly golden. Cool slightly.
◇ Trim the asparagus and blanch in boiling water for 2 minutes. Drain, rinse under cold water, and pat dry. Reserve 8 tips and chop the remainder.

◇ Sprinkle the chopped asparagus, Gorgonzola and basil into the pastry shell, beat together the cream and eggs and pour over. Arrange the asparagus tips attractively over the filling and sprinkle with the Parmesan.
◇ Lower the oven temperature to 375°F and bake for 25-30 minutes, until golden and set.

BEET, TARRAGON & GINGER SALAD

~

In my opinion, beets are a much underrated vegetable. If you have time, cook the beets yourself for this recipe: bake them for 1½-2 hours at 350°F, loosely covered with foil.

2 POUNDS COOKED BEETS (SEE ABOVE)

DRESSING

4 TABLESPOONS HAZELNUT OIL

1 TABLESPOON BALSAMIC VINEGAR

2 TEASPOONS CHOPPED FRESH TARRAGON

1 TEASPOON GRATED FRESH ROOT GINGER

SALT AND PEPPER

TO SERVE

1 BUNCH SCALLIONS, TRIMMED AND THICKLY SLICED

¾ CUP HAZELNUTS, TOASTED

TO GARNISH

TARRAGON SPRIGS (OPTIONAL)

◇ Peel the cooked beets if necessary, and cut into wedges. Place in a plastic container.
◇ Blend the dressing ingredients together and pour over the beets. Toss well, cover and chill several hours.
◇ Toss with the scallions and sprinkle the hazelnuts over just before serving.

TOP *Gorgonzola & asparagus quiche*
BOTTOM *Beet, tarragon & ginger salad*

SALMON & DILL PIE

~

Pies are always popular on picnics. This particularly pretty one tastes as good as it looks.

====

PASTRY

1½ CUPS ALL-PURPOSE FLOUR

½ TEASPOON SALT

½ CUP UNSALTED BUTTER, DICED

1 EGG YOLK

1 TABLESPOON COLD WATER

FILLING

8 OUNCES SMOKED SALMON

3 EGGS

1¼ CUPS SOUR CREAM

3 TABLESPOONS CHOPPED FRESH DILL

1 TABLESPOON WHOLEGRAIN MUSTARD

1 TABLESPOON LEMON JUICE

PEPPER

====

◇ Make the pastry: sift the flour and salt together into a bowl and cut in the butter until the mixture resembles fine breadcrumbs. Make a well in the center and work in the egg yolk and water to form a firm paste. Wrap and chill for 30 minutes.

◇ Roll out the dough on a lightly floured surface and use to line a deep 9-inch fluted pie pan. Prick the base with a fork and chill for a further 15 minutes.

◇ Line pastry with foil and fill with dried beans. Bake in a preheated oven at 400°F for 10 minutes. Remove the beans and foil and bake for 10-12 minutes more, until the pastry is crisp and lightly golden. Remove the pastry shell from the oven and cool.

◇ Coarsely chop the salmon and sprinkle over the cooled pastry shell. Beat the remaining ingredients together until combined, and pour over the salmon.

◇ Bake the pie for 25 minutes, until golden and firm in the center. Remove from the oven and chill.

◇ Transport the pie in a cooler and serve cut into wedges.

SMOKED TROUT PASTE

~

Serve this creamy trout paste with a selection of crackers or French bread.

====

8 OUNCES SMOKED TROUT FILLETS

½ CUP RICOTTA CHEESE

3 TABLESPOONS CREAMED HORSERADISH SAUCE

1 TABLESPOON CHOPPED FRESH CHIVES

1 TABLESPOON BRANDY (OPTIONAL)

JUICE OF 1 LEMON

2 TABLESPOONS LIGHT CREAM OR FROMAGE FRAIS

PEPPER

====

◇ Coarsely chop the trout and purée in a food processor with all the remaining ingredients, except the cream, until smooth. Stir in the cream and adjust seasoning.

◇ Transfer to a container and chill until required.

◇ Serve with slices of French bread or crackers.

LEFT *Salmon & dill pie*
RIGHT *Smoked trout paste*

COUNTRY CHICKEN, HAM & HERB TERRINE

~

A rich chicken and herb mousse is layered alternately with strips of ham and whole chicken breast, set, and unmolded to reveal an array of herbs

1 12-OUNCE SLICE FULLY-COOKED HAM

1½ POUNDS CHICKEN BREAST FILLETS, SKINNED

1¼ CUPS CHICKEN STOCK

1 TABLESPOON OLIVE OIL

1 SMALL ONION, MINCED

1 CLOVE GARLIC, CRUSHED

1 EGG, SEPARATED

JUICE OF 1 LEMON

PINCH OF APPLE PIE SPICE

⅔ CUP HEAVY CREAM

1½ ENVELOPES POWDERED GELATIN

⅔ CUP SHELLED PISTACHIO NUTS

2 TABLESPOONS CHOPPED HERBS (PARSLEY, TARRAGON, THYME)

SALT AND PEPPER

TO GARNISH

A SELECTION OF PRETTY HERBS

◇ Trim fat from ham and cut into ¼-inch strips.
◇ Poach 2 chicken breasts in the stock for 12-15 minutes. Drain and cool. Reserve 3 tablespoons of stock.
◇ Finely chop the remaining chicken. Heat the oil and sauté the chopped chicken with the onion and garlic for 6-8 minutes, until cooked. Cool.
◇ Lightly oil a 2-pound loaf pan, and lay fresh herbs over the base, pressing them down lightly. Set aside.
◇ Purée the chicken and onion with the egg yolk, lemon juice, mixed spice and salt and pepper until very smooth. Turn into a bowl and stir in the cream.
◇ Heat the gelatin gently in the reserved poaching stock until dissolved. Stir in a spoonful of chicken purée, then stir the gelatin mixture into the remaining purée. Stir in the nuts and chopped herbs.
◇ Whisk the egg white until stiff and fold into the chicken mixture, until incorporated. Spoon a shallow layer of the chicken mousse mixture into the base of the prepared pan, spreading very carefully over the herbs without moving them. Layer the strips of ham, chicken breast and chicken mousse into the pan, finishing with the mousse. Tap to dislodge holes, smooth and chill until set.

SUMMER GREENS SALAD

~

Use a selection of your favorite salad leaves and herbs for this light and fragrant salad.

DRESSING

4 TABLESPOONS EXTRA VIRGIN OLIVE OIL

2 TEASPOONS RASPBERRY OR OTHER FRUIT VINEGAR

1 TEASPOON WHOLEGRAIN MUSTARD

½ TEASPOON CLEAR HONEY

SALT AND PEPPER

SALAD

6 LARGE HANDFULS OF MIXED SUMMER GREENS (COS, FRISEE [CURLY ENDIVE], LEAF LETTUCE, ROSSO, OAK LEAF, RADICCHIO, ROCKET, MÂCHE)

6 TABLESPOONS CHOPPED HERBS (BASIL CHERVIL, CHIVES, LEMON BALM, MINT, TARRAGON, THYME)

2 TABLESPOONS SUNFLOWER SEEDS, TOASTED

EDIBLE FLOWERS (BORAGE, NASTURTIUMS, PANSIES, ROSE PETALS, VIOLAS)

◇ Blend the dressing ingredients together, and place in a screw-top jar. Mix all the salad ingredients together in a large bowl, shake the dressing to combine the oil and vinegar, and pour over the salad. Scatter over the flowers, toss well and serve immediately.

TOP *Country chicken, ham & herb terrine*
BOTTOM *Summer greens salad*

PISSALADIÈRE

~

Try this tasty variation of the classic Niçoise pizza. The dough is spread with olive paste and topped with sweet onions, anchovies, thyme and olives. Olive paste is available from most good supermarkets and delicatessens.

TOPPING

2 TABLESPOONS OLIVE OIL

1½ POUNDS ONIONS, THINLY SLICED

2 CLOVES GARLIC, CRUSHED

1 TABLESPOON CHOPPED FRESH THYME

1 TEASPOON FENNEL SEEDS

1 2-OUNCE CAN ANCHOVY FILLETS, DRAINED

A LITTLE MILK

1 TABLESPOON OLIVE PASTE

8-12 PITTED BLACK OLIVES

DOUGH

1¾ CUPS ALL-PURPOSE FLOUR

1 TEASPOON FAST-ACTING DRIED YEAST

½ TEASPOON SALT

2 TABLESPOONS OLIVE OIL

½-⅔ CUP TEPID WATER

GLAZE

1 EGG YOLK, BEATEN WITH 1 TABLESPOON
MILK AND A PINCH OF SALT

◇ Heat the oil and sauté the onions, garlic, thyme and fennel seeds for 20-25 minutes, until the onions are softened and lightly golden. Stir from time to time to stop the onions from burning, as they will become bitter.

◇ Soak the anchovy fillets in a little milk for 10 minutes, to remove the saltiness, drain and pat dry. Set aside.

◇ Prepare the dough: combine the flour, yeast and salt in a large bowl, make a well in the center and work in the oil and enough warm water to form a pliable dough. Knead on a lightly floured surface for 5 minutes, until smooth and elastic. Place the dough in a lightly oiled bowl, brush the surface with oil and cover with plastic wrap. Let rise in a warm place until doubled in size.

◇ Punch down the dough and roll out on a lightly floured surface to a 10-inch round and place on a greased baking sheet or pizza pan. Prick the base with a fork.

◇ Spread the dough with the olive paste and top with the onion mixture, anchovies and olives. With a sharp knife, cut small slits all around the edge of the dough to make an attractive finish. Brush with a little glaze and drizzle the onion mixture with oil and bake in a preheated oven at 475°F for 25 minutes, until golden.

◇ Allow to cool and serve cut into wedges, with a spoonful of crème fraîche, if desired.

◇ For a tasty alternative, substitute 3 tablespoons drained, sun-dried tomatoes in oil for the anchovy fillets.

Pissaladière

BEEF & HERB ROULADE

~

This is my version of the Sicilian dish Farso Magro, a rolled, stuffed rump steak, served cold cut into slices. This recipe serves 8-10. Ask your butcher to cut you a steak from the widest part of the rump.

═══

2 POUNDS BEEF SIRLOIN STEAK

FILLING

6 OUNCES PROSCIUTTO SLICED THICKLY

12 OUNCES LEAN GROUND BEEF

2 CLOVES GARLIC, CRUSHED

⅓ CUP PITTED GREEN OLIVES

3 TABLESPOONS FRESHLY GRATED PARMESAN CHEESE

¾ CUP FRESH WHITE BREADCRUMBS

2 TABLESPOONS CHOPPED FRESH HERBS (BASIL, OREGANO, SAGE AND THYME)

1 TABLESPOON CAPERS, FINELY CHOPPED

2 SMALL EGGS, LIGHTLY BEATEN

SALT AND PEPPER

2 TABLESPOONS OLIVE OIL

═══

◇ Trim any fat from the steak and place between 2 sheets of wax paper. Beat gently with a rolling pin to flatten to ½ inch thick. Discard the paper and cover the steak with the slices of ham.

◇ Mix all the remaining ingredients together, except the oil, seasoning well. Spread the mixture over the ham, leaving a narrow border round the edge of the steak.

◇ Roll up the steak from one long side, tucking the ends under as you go, to seal in the filling. Tie up with string securely, but not too tightly.

◇ Heat the oil in a large skillet and brown the beef on all sides. Wrap loosely in foil, place in a roasting pan and cook in a preheated oven at 400°F for 1 hour. Remove from the oven. Leave in the foil and chill thoroughly.

◇ Wrap in wax paper and transport in a cooler.

ONION & PEPPER RELISH

~

An excellent accompaniment to cold meats and pies, which can be made in advance and stored in a screw-top jar.

═══

1 LARGE RED SWEET PEPPER

8 OUNCES PEARL ONIONS

1 TABLESPOON OLIVE OIL

2 CLOVES GARLIC, PEELED

1 TEASPOON MUSTARD SEEDS

1 TEASPOON CHOPPED FRESH THYME

1 CINNAMON STICK

6 WHOLE CLOVES

5 TABLESPOONS WATER

2 TABLESPOONS TOMATO PASTE

2 TABLESPOONS BALSAMIC VINEGAR

2 TABLESPOONS SUGAR

1 BAYLEAF

½ TEASPOON SALT

PEPPER

═══

◇ Place the pepper under a hot broiler until the skin becomes charred and blistered, turning frequently. Wrap in a plastic bag and let cool for 30 minutes.

◇ Blanch the onions in boiling water for 1 minute. Drain, then rinse under cold water. Peel and cut in half.

◇ Heat the oil in a heavy-based pan and fry the onions, garlic, mustard seeds and thyme for 5 minutes, until the onions are brown. Add the remaining ingredients, cover and simmer for 10 minutes.

◇ Peel the cooled pepper over a bowl to catch any juices. Discard the seeds. Cut the flesh into thin strips and add to the pan with the juices.

◇ Remove the pan from the heat and let the relish cool. Spoon into a screw-top jar and chill to store.

LEFT *Beef & herb roulade*
RIGHT *Onion & pepper relish*

PEAR & CARDAMOM TATIN

~

This wickedly delicious upside-down pie is best eaten the same day, with a spoonful of crème fraîche.

PASTRY

1¼ CUPS ALL-PURPOSE FLOUR

½ TEASPOON SALT

¾ CUP UNSALTED BUTTER, DICED

¼ CUP FINELY GROUND WALNUTS

2 TEASPOONS SUPERFINE SUGAR

1 EGG YOLK

CARAMEL

⅓ CUP UNSALTED BUTTER

⅓ CUP SUPERFINE SUGAR

3 CARDAMOM PODS

TOPPING

3 POUNDS FIRM PEARS, PEELED, HALVED AND CORED

⅓ CUP WALNUT HALVES

◇ To make the pastry, sift the flour and salt into a large bowl. Cut in the butter until the mixture resembles fine breadcrumbs. Stir in the walnuts and sugar and work in the egg yolk and 1 tablespoon cold water to form a soft dough. Wrap and chill for 20 minutes.

◇ Melt the butter and sugar in an 8-9-inch oven-proof skillet. Remove seeds from the cardamom pods, crush them and add to the skillet. Boil for 5 minutes. Add the pears, cut side up. Cook for 5 minutes, or until the pears begin to brown underneath. Add walnut halves.

◇ Roll out the chilled pastry to a circle a little larger than the skillet. Cover the pears with the pastry, pressing it up the sides of the skillet.

◇ Transfer to a preheated oven at 400°F and bake for 20 minutes, until golden.

◇ Leave in the skillet for 5 minutes and invert onto a large plate. Let cool.

CARAMELIZED ORANGES

~

Whole fresh oranges are served with a boozy citrus sauce and decorated with ripe cherries to make this attractive chilled summer dessert.

8 LARGE ORANGES

¾ CUP GRANULATED SUGAR

5 TABLESPOONS WATER

JUICE 1 LEMON

6 OUNCES CHERRIES ON STEMS

2 TABLESPOONS GRAND MARNIER

TO DECORATE

LEMON BALM LEAVES

◇ Peel 6 of the oranges, removing all the pith, and set aside. Peel the 2 remaining oranges, leaving the pith on, and cut the peel into thin strips. Blanch the strips in boiling water for 2 minutes, drain, rinse under cold water and pat dry. Halve the 2 semi-peeled oranges and squeeze the juice into a bowl.

◇ Heat the sugar gently until dissolved, add the water, orange juice and lemon juice and boil rapidly for 3 minutes until thick and syrupy. Add the peeled oranges to the pan, turning them to coat them with syrup. Remove the oranges to a shallow dish, surround them with the cherries, and set aside to cool.

◇ Add the strips of peel to the syrup and boil rapidly for 4-5 minutes, until the peel begins to caramelize. Remove from the heat and pour in the Grand Marnier.

◇ Pour the syrup and caramelized peel over the oranges and cherries. Let cool and chill for several hours or overnight, spooning over the sauce occasionally.

◇ Serve decorated with lemon balm leaves if desired.

TOP *Pear & cardamom tatin*
BOTTOM *Caramelized oranges*

LEMON CHEESECAKE WITH SUMMER BERRY SAUCE

~

A tangy lemon cheesecake made with a low-fat cream cheese and fromage frais. A purée of summer berries makes the perfect sauce.

════

BASE

1⅓ CUPS CRUSHED VANILLA WAFERS

¼ CUP UNSALTED BUTTER, MELTED

FILLING

1 CUP LOW-FAT CREAM CHEESE

1 CUP YOGURT OR FROMAGE FRAIS

⅓ CUP SUPERFINE SUGAR

2 EGGS

RIND AND JUICE OF 1 LARGE LEMON

3 TABLESPOONS ALL-PURPOSE FLOUR

½ TEASPOON APPLE PIE SPICE

SAUCE

1 POUND MIXED SUMMER BERRIES

2 TABLESPOONS SUGAR

2 TABLESPOONS CASSIS

TO DECORATE

SUMMER BERRIES

════

◇ Grease, and line the sides of, a 7-inch springform cake pan.
◇ Make the base: stir the crushed cookies into the melted butter until well coated, and press into the base of the prepared pan. Chill for 15 minutes.
◇ Meanwhile, prepare the filling: beat all the ingredients together until smooth. Pour the mixture over the chilled crumb base and bake in a preheated oven at 350°F for 45-50 minutes, until just firm in the center. Remove from the oven, cover with a clean dish towel and let cool in the pan and chill.
◇ Make the sauce: reserve ½-¾ cup mixed berries for decoration. Hull any strawberries and discard the stems from any currants and wash all the fruit well. Place in a pan with the sugar and cassis and simmer gently for 5 minutes, until the fruit is soft. Purée until smooth and pass through a sieve to remove the seeds. Set aside to cool and transfer to a screw-top jar and chill.

SPICED APPLE & BLUEBERRY MUFFINS

~

Quick to make, these fruit muffins are delicious with crème fraîche or yogurt. This recipe makes 12 large muffins.

════

MUFFINS

1¾ CUPS ALL-PURPOSE FLOUR

1 TABLESPOON BAKING POWDER

⅓ CUP SUPERFINE SUGAR

1 TEASPOON APPLE PIE SPICE

PINCH OF SALT

½ CUP UNSALTED BUTTER, MELTED

1 EGG, LIGHTLY BEATEN

¾ CUP MILK

1 EATING APPLE, PEELED, CORED AND CHOPPED

¾ CUP BLUEBERRIES

════

◇ Place the flour, baking powder, sugar, apple pie spice, salt, butter, egg and milk in a food processor and blend until smooth.
◇ Transfer to a bowl and stir in the apple and blueberries until evenly combined. Spoon into a lightly oiled muffin pan and bake in a preheated oven at 425°F for 15-20 minutes, until risen and golden.
◇ Remove from the oven, cool in the pan for 5 minutes, and turn out on to a wire rack to cool.

FRONT *Lemon cheesecake with summer berry sauce*
BACK *Spiced apple & blueberry muffins*

PEACH NECTAR

~

Crème de peche is a peach liqueur from France, and is quite delicious, especially when blended with chilled white wine and mixed with sparkling mineral water. If the peach liqueur is unavailable, substitute brandy and stir in 1 tablespoon clear honey.

1 BOTTLE CHILLED DRY WHITE WINE

½ CUP CRÈME DE PECHE

1 RIPE PEACH, PITTED AND THINLY SLICED

2½ CUPS SPARKLING MINERAL WATER

TO SERVE

ICE CUBES

◇ Pour the wine into a large jug, add the crème de peche, peach slices and the sparkling water.
◇ Add a few ice cubes and serve immediately.

RASPBERRY & GINGER CORDIAL

~

A deliciously refreshing summer cordial, colorful and fragrant, it makes the perfect non-alcoholic aperitif. If you prefer, use sparkling wine instead of mineral water.

CORDIAL

1 POUND RASPBERRIES

6 TABLESPOONS CLEAR HONEY

JUICE OF 1 LEMON

2 TEASPOONS GROUND GINGER

TO SERVE

CRUSHED ICE

SPARKLING MINERAL WATER

◇ Purée the raspberries, honey, lemon juice and ginger together, in a food processor or blender, until smooth. Pass through a fine sieve to remove the seeds.
◇ Pour into a screw-top jar or bottle and chill.
◇ Divide the cordial between 6 glasses, add crushed ice, and mineral water to fill the glasses. Serve immediately.

SOUTHERN MINT JULEP

~

A deliciously refreshing minted whiskey cocktail. Serve decorated with extra mint leaves.

MINT SYRUP

1 LARGE LEMON

1 TABLESPOON SUGAR

6 SPRIGS MINT, BRUISED

1¼ CUPS BOILING WATER

TO SERVE

1 HANDFUL MINT LEAVES, CRUSHED

6 TABLESPOONS WHISKEY

6 TEASPOONS CONFECTIONERS' SUGAR

CRUSHED ICE

MINT SPRIGS (OPTIONAL)

◇ Make the syrup: slice the lemon thickly and place in a bowl with the sugar and mint sprigs. Pour in the boiling water and let stand for 4 hours or overnight.
◇ Strain into a screw-top jar or bottle and keep cool.
◇ To serve: place 2 tablespoons of mint syrup into each glass and add a few crushed mint leaves, 1 tablespoon whiskey, and 1 teaspoon sugar to each one. Add crushed ice, stir well and decorate with mint sprigs.

RIGHT *Peach nectar*
LEFT *Raspberry & ginger cordial*
CENTER *Southern mint julep*

DINING ALFRESCO

The recipes in 'Dining Alfresco' are among the most elaborate; since the meals are meant to be served outside at home, it is easier for you to prepare more lavish dishes. At the same time, they have been created so that you have plenty of time to spend outside with your guests, rather than labor over preparations in the kitchen. Most of the dishes can be made in advance and are served chilled. Others are served warm or hot and only need to be popped into the oven or under the broiler just before serving. Since the kitchen is nearby, there is no need to worry about transporting the food, but you will probably want to save room in the refrigerator for any dishes that need to be kept cold until they are required.

This can be an occasion to use your most elegant china, glasses, cutlery and linen; but it is just as enjoyable to take a more casual approach and relax around an informal table, indulging in a selection of delicious and imaginative recipes – while enjoying the fresh outdoors. These recipes have been created for you to easily put together a complete menu of spectacular, fresh food to grace a truly memorable alfresco lunch or dinner party.

CONTENTS

Smoked salmon phyllo tartlets
Fresh pea and lettuce soup 88

Radicchio with broiled chèvre cheese
Prosciutto salad...90

Scallop and mussel escabeche 92

Stuffed onions with sun-dried tomatoes
Warm pasta pommodoro...94

Spinach and ricotta pie
Watercress roulade with smoked haddock...96

Spiced chicken with tabbouleh molds
Oven-baked eggplant salad..98

Pork medley 100

Salmon and sole ceviche
B.L.T. salad..102

Tiramisu with raspberries
Gingerbread 104

Plum, Sauterne and cinnamon ice cream
Spiced braised pears...106

Citrus ice-cream sherbet
Iced mocha coffee
Champagne sunset 108

SMOKED SALMON PHYLLO TARTLETS

~

A salad of smoked salmon, asparagus tips, hard-cooked eggs and rocket, served in phyllo shells with a piquant shallot dressing, makes an attractive and elegant appetizer.

1 10-OUNCE PACKET PHYLLO PASTRY SHEETS

¼ CUP UNSALTED BUTTER, MELTED

24 ASPARAGUS TIPS

5 SMALL EGGS, HARD-COOKED

6 OUNCES SMOKED SALMON

1 CUP ROCKET

DRESSING

6 TABLESPOONS EXTRA VIRGIN OLIVE OIL

3 TABLESPOONS SOUR CREAM

4 TEASPOONS SHERRY VINEGAR

1 TABLESPOON CHOPPED FRESH DILL

SALT AND PEPPER

TO GARNISH

DILL SPRIGS

◇ Cut the phyllo pastry into 24×5-inch squares.
◇ Lightly butter 6×4½-inch tartlet pans and lay 4 squares of pastry in each one, brushing the pastry with melted butter. Press gently into the edges to form 6 star-shaped phyllo pastry shells. The ends of the pastry will stick up above the tops of pans. Leave for 30 minutes to allow the pastry to firm up.
◇ Bake in a preheated oven at 350°F for 15-20 minutes, until crisp and golden. Cool slightly and carefully lift the pastry shells out of the pans and cool on a wire rack.
◇ Prepare the salad filling: blanch the asparagus tips in boiling water for 1 minute. Drain, rinse under cold water and pat dry.
◇ Peel and quarter the cooked eggs.

◇ Cut the salmon into thin strips.
◇ Wash and dry the rocket.
◇ Blend all the dressing ingredients together.
◇ Arrange the asparagus, eggs, salmon and rocket in the phyllo shells, spoon over the dressing, garnish and serve.

FRESH PEA & LETTUCE SOUP

~

A light and delicate summer soup that can be served hot or cold. If serving cold, leave the soup to cool, then stir in ⅔ cup yogurt and chill for 2 hours.

1 TABLESPOON OLIVE OIL

1 ONION, FINELY CHOPPED

1 SMALL HEAD LETTUCE

2 POUNDS FRESH PEAS, SHELLED

2 TABLESPOONS CHOPPED FRESH MINT

3 CUPS VEGETABLE STOCK

JUICE OF 1 LEMON

SALT AND PEPPER

TO GARNISH

A LITTLE YOGURT

BASIL LEAVES

◇ Heat the oil and sauté the onion for 5 minutes.
◇ Wash and dry the lettuce, discarding any tough outer leaves, and slice thinly. Add to the pan with the peas and mint. Stir once and add the stock, lemon juice and seasonings. Bring to a boil, cover and simmer gently for 15-20 minutes, until the peas are cooked.
◇ Purée the soup in a food processor or blender and serve at once with a swirl of yogurt and basil leaves.

BACK *Smoked salmon phyllo tartlets*
FRONT *Fresh pea & lettuce soup*

RADICCHIO WITH BROILED CHÈVRE CHEESE

~

The slightly bitter flavor of the radicchio is complemented with the creamy, melted chèvre cheese and sweet char-broiled pepper.

3 RED SWEET PEPPERS

6 OUNCES CHÈVRE CHEESE

⅔ CUP HAZELNUT OIL

4 TEASPOONS BALSAMIC VINEGAR

6 SPRIGS ROSEMARY, BRUISED

6 ROUNDS FRENCH BREAD

1 CLOVE GARLIC, HALVED

1 SMALL RADICCHIO

2 TABLESPOONS HAZELNUTS, TOASTED AND CHOPPED

PEPPER

◇ Place the peppers under a hot broiler until the skins are charred and blistered, turning frequently. Remove from heat and place in a plastic bag for 30 minutes to soften.
◇ Cut the chèvre cheese into 6 thin slices and place in a shallow dish. Blend the oil and vinegar together and pour over the cheese. Add the rosemary, cover and chill to marinate for several hours.
◇ Trim the French bread to the same size as the cheese and toast lightly on both sides. Rub all over with the garlic and set aside.
◇ Peel the peppers over a bowl to catch the juices. Discard the seeds, cut the flesh into thick strips and set aside.
◇ Remove the cheese from the marinade and sit on top of the toasted bread. Discard all but 1 sprig of rosemary. Chop the leaves finely, then return to the oil and vinegar.
◇ Wash the radicchio and separate the leaves. Arrange a few leaves and the peppers on 6 serving plates.
◇ Broil the cheese croûtons for 1-2 minutes until the cheese just melts and place 1 on each plate. Drizzle over the marinade and sprinkle over the toasted hazelnuts.

PROSCIUTTO SALAD

~

In this pretty salad, thin slices of Italian ham and fresh figs are served with a mixture of ricotta and fresh herbs, formed into small egg shapes.

SALAD

1 TABLESPOON CHOPPED FRESH HERBS (BASIL, FENNEL, OREGANO, TARRAGON)

½ CLOVE GARLIC, CRUSHED

1 CUP RICOTTA CHEESE

6 OUNCES PROSCIUTTO SLICES

6 RIPE FIGS

DRESSING

4 TABLESPOONS EXTRA VIRGIN OLIVE OIL

1 TABLESPOON RASPBERRY OR OTHER FRUIT VINEGAR

PINCH OF SUGAR

SALT AND PEPPER

TO GARNISH

A SELECTION OF FRESH HERB LEAVES

◇ Stir the herbs and garlic into the ricotta until combined. Using 2 teaspoons, pass a spoonful of the mixture from 1 to the other to form a small egg shape. Repeat to make 18 mounds. Chill until required.
◇ Cut each fig into 3 wedges.
◇ Arrange the slices of prosciutto on a large serving plate and arrange the ricotta mounds and fig wedges attractively over the top.
◇ Blend the dressing ingredients together and drizzle over the salad. Garnish and serve at once.

FRONT *Radicchio with broiled chèvre cheese*
BACK *Prosciutto salad*

SCALLOP & MUSSEL ESCABECHE

~

Escabeche is a dish of cooked fish or meat chilled and marinated in oil, vinegar, herbs and spices. This is an adaptation of a Spanish recipe. If possible serve this elegant appetizer in scallop shells.

═

POACHING LIQUID

1 TABLESPOON OLIVE OIL

1 SMALL ONION, CHOPPED

1 CLOVE GARLIC, CRUSHED

⅔ CUP DRY WHITE WINE

⅔ CUP WATER

GRATED RIND AND JUICE OF 1 LIME

2 SPRIGS ROSEMARY, BRUISED

12 LARGE SCALLOPS

MARINADE

5 – 6 TABLESPOONS LIGHT OLIVE OIL

JUICE OF 1 LIME

1 TABLESPOON CHOPPED FRESH PARSLEY

2 TEASPOONS CHOPPED FRESH ROSEMARY

1 TEASPOON CORIANDER SEEDS, CRUSHED

PINCH OF SUGAR

PINCH OF CAYENNE PEPPER

SALT AND PEPPER

18 RAW MUSSELS IN SHELLS, SCRUBBED

TO GARNISH

LIME SLICES

PARSLEY SPRIGS

═

◇ Heat the oil and sauté the onion and garlic for 5 minutes. Add the wine, water, lime rind and juice and rosemary. Bring to a boil and simmer gently, covered, for 10 minutes.

◇ Wash and dry the scallops and cut away the tough membrane. Slice each scallop in half, horizontally, and poach in the liquid, over a very low heat, for 1-2 minutes, until they become opaque. Do not over-cook or the scallops will be tough. Remove with a slotted spoon and transfer to a shallow dish. Reserve the poaching liquid.

◇ Blend all the marinade ingredients together and pour over the scallops.

◇ Strain the reserved poaching liquid and add 5 tablespoons to the scallops. Set aside to marinate.

◇ Reduce the remaining liquid in a large pan until only about 3 tablespoons remain. Add the mussels to the pan, cover and cook for 4-5 minutes, until all the mussel shells are open and the mussels are cooked. Discard any that do not open.

◇ Carefully remove the mussels from their shells, reserving 18 half shells. Add the mussels to the scallops and chill for 1-2 hours or longer.

◇ Serve the scallops and mussels and marinade in individual dishes or scallop shells, sitting the mussels back in their half shells, if liked. Garnish with lime slices and parsley. Serve with crusty bread.

Scallop & mussel escabeche

STUFFED ONIONS WITH SUN-DRIED TOMATOES

~

The intense flavor of the sun-dried tomatoes combined with creamy chèvre cheese and pinenuts, makes this a truly delicious stuffing, which can be prepared in advance.

3 LARGE RED ONIONS, UNPEELED

FILLING

⅔ CUP SUN-DRIED TOMATOES IN OIL, DRAINED

4 OUNCES CHÈVRE CHEESE

1 CLOVE GARLIC, CRUSHED

¾ CUP FRESH WHITE BREADCRUMBS

¼ CUP PINENUTS, TOASTED

1 TABLESPOON CHOPPED FRESH BASIL

1 TEASPOON CHOPPED FRESH THYME

1 EGG

SALT AND PEPPER

TO SERVE

SALAD GARNISH

CRÈME FRAÎCHE

◇ Place the unpeeled onions in a large pan and cover with cold water. Bring to the boil, and cook for 15 minutes, until tender. Drain the onions and cool.

◇ Prepare the filling: slice the tomatoes thinly and place in a large bowl. Cube the cheese and add to tomatoes with the remaining ingredients, except the egg and set aside.

◇ Cut the cooled onions in half, through the root and tip, and carefully remove most of the cooked onion, leaving 1 or 2 layers to keep the shape and form the empty shells.

◇ Discard half of the flesh, finely chop the rest and stir into the filling. Lightly beat the egg and stir into the filling. Spoon into the empty shells, packing the mixture in well, and place in a heatproof dish.

◇ Bake in a preheated oven at 400°F for 20-25 minutes, until bubbling and golden.

◇ Serve the onions hot as an appetizer.

WARM PASTA POMMODORO

~

This is an unusual pasta dish, in that the hot pasta is tossed in an uncooked tomato sauce and served while still warm. This gives a wonderfully fresh tasting sauce, ideal for a summer evening.

3 POUNDS RIPE TOMATOES

⅓ CUP SUN-DRIED TOMATOES IN OIL, DRAINED AND THINLY SLICED

½ CUP PITTED BLACK OLIVES, HALVED

GRATED RIND AND JUICE OF 1 LEMON

2 TABLESPOONS CHOPPED FRESH BASIL

⅔ CUP VIRGIN OLIVE OIL

1 POUND 2 OUNCES FRESH LINGUINE OR TAGLIATELLE

1 CLOVE GARLIC, CHOPPED

1 SMALL DRIED RED CHILLI, DE-SEEDED AND CRUSHED

1 TEASPOON CHOPPED FRESH THYME

⅔ CUP CHOPPED WALNUTS, TOASTED

SALT AND PEPPER

TO GARNISH

BASIL LEAVES

◇ Peel and seed the tomatoes and chop. Place in a large bowl and stir in the sun-dried tomatoes, olives, lemon rind and juice, basil and 2 tablespoons olive oil. Cover and chill for 1-2 hours.

◇ Just before serving, cook the pasta in boiling salted water for 2-3 minutes, until 'al dente' (just done).

◇ Meanwhile, heat the remaining oil in a large skillet and sauté the garlic, chilli and thyme until golden. Remove the skillet from the heat.

◇ Drain the cooked pasta and toss with the oil and garlic. Stir in the tomato sauce and walnuts and serve immediately. Garnish with basil leaves and sprinkle with Parmesan, if desired.

RIGHT *Stuffed onions with sun-dried tomatoes*
LEFT *Warm pasta pommodoro*

SPINACH & RICOTTA PIE

PASTRY

1¼ CUPS ALL-PURPOSE FLOUR

3 TABLESPOONS FRESHLY GRATED PARMESAN

PINCH OF SALT

½ CUP BUTTER, DICED

1 EGG YOLK

FILLING

1 TABLESPOON OLIVE OIL

2 LEEKS, TRIMMED AND THINLY SLICED

1 CLOVE GARLIC, CRUSHED

1 TABLESPOON CHOPPED FRESH THYME

4 CUPS SHREDDED SPINACH LEAVES

1 CUP RICOTTA CHEESE

3 EGGS, LIGHTLY BEATEN

⅔ CUP LIGHT CREAM

PINCH OF FRESHLY GRATED NUTMEG

¼ CUP PINENUTS

SALT AND PEPPER

◇ Combine the flour, Parmesan and salt in a bowl and cut in the butter. Stir in the egg yolk and 1 tablespoon cold water to form a firm paste. Cover and chill for 30 minutes.
◇ Roll out the dough and use to line a 9-inch fluted pie pan and prick the base. Chill for a further 15 minutes.
◇ Line pastry with foil and fill with dried beans. Bake in a preheated oven at 400°F for 8 minutes. Remove the baking beans and foil and bake 10-12 minutes more, until the dough is crisp and golden. Remove from the oven and leave to cool. Reduce the oven temperature to 375°F.
◇ Heat the oil in a large skillet and sauté the leeks, garlic and thyme for 5 minutes. Add the spinach and stir for 1-2 minutes. Leave to cool slightly.
◇ Cream together the ricotta, eggs and cream until smooth and stir in the seasonings.
◇ Drain the spinach mixture, pressing out as much liquid as possible, and spread over the pastry shell. Pour in the cheese mixture and sprinkle over the nuts. Bake for 30-35 minutes until lightly golden and set.

WATERCRESS ROULADE WITH SMOKED HADDOCK

8 OUNCES SMOKED HADDOCK FILLETS

1¼ CUPS MILK

4 CUPS WATERCRESS

¼ CUP BUTTER

5 TABLESPOONS ALL-PURPOSE FLOUR

3 EGGS, SEPARATED

½ CUP GRATED GRUYÈRE CHEESE

FILLING

SCANT 1 CUP CREAM CHEESE

2 TABLESPOONS CHOPPED FRESH HERBS

3 TABLESPOONS GROUND ALMONDS

3 TABLESPOONS PARMESAN, GRATED

1 TABLESPOON LEMON JUICE

½ TEASPOON GROUND MACE

SALT AND PEPPER

◇ Line a 9×13-inch jelly roll pan with parchment paper.
◇ Poach the haddock fillets in the milk for 6-8 minutes, until cooked. Drain and reserve the fish and stock.
◇ Wash and dry the watercress and remove the stalks. Chop finely and place in a large bowl.
◇ Melt the butter, stir in the flour and cook for 1 minute. Add stock and cook, stirring until thickened.
◇ Remove from the heat, cool slightly and beat in the egg yolks and cheese. Blend with the watercress and season.
◇ Whisk the egg whites until stiff and fold into the mixture, until combined. Spoon into the prepared pan, smooth the surface and bake in a preheated oven at 400°F for 20-25 minutes, until risen and set. Remove from the oven, cover with a clean dish cloth and chill.
◇ Skin and flake the haddock, and blend with the cream cheese and all remaining ingredients. When the roulade is cold, turn it out on to the dish cloth, peel off the paper and spread over the filling. Roll up tightly and serve sliced.

TOP *Spinach & ricotta pie*
BOTTOM *Watercress roulade with smoked haddock*

SPICED CHICKEN WITH TABBOULEH MOLDS

===

1½ POUNDS SKINLESS CHICKEN BREAST

2 TABLESPOONS OLIVE OIL

1 CLOVE GARLIC, CRUSHED

1 TEASPOON GROUND CUMIN

½ TEASPOON APPLE PIE SPICE

PINCH OF CHILLI POWDER

TABBOULEH

1¾ CUPS BULGUR

1 SMALL RED ONION, FINELY DICED

1 RIPE TOMATO, SEEDED AND FINELY DICED

1 PEACH, PITTED AND FINELY DICED

½ SMALL CUCUMBER, PEELED, SEEDED AND FINELY DICED

⅓ CUP CURRANTS

2 TABLESPOONS CHOPPED FRESH MINT

1 TABLESPOON CHOPPED FRESH CILANTRO

DRESSING

½ CUP VIRGIN OLIVE OIL

JUICE OF 1 LIME

½ TEASPOON HONEY

SALT AND PEPPER

===

◇ Cut the chicken into thin strips. Heat the oil and stir-fry the strips over a high heat for 2-3 minutes, until browned on all sides. Add the garlic and spices, lower the heat and sauté for 2-3 minutes, until the chicken is cooked through. Remove from the heat and set aside to chill.
◇ Soak the bulgur in cold water for 15 minutes. Drain well, pressing out as much liquid as possible. Pat dry. Place in a bowl and stir in the remaining ingredients.
◇ Blend the dressing ingredients together and stir ¾ into the salad until evenly combined. Spoon the mixture into 6 lightly oiled ¾-cup molds, pressing firmly, and cover and chill.
◇ Remove the molds from the refrigerator 15 minutes before serving. Unmold onto plates and surround with the spiced chicken, drizzle over the dressing and garnish.

OVEN-BAKED EGGPLANT SALAD

===

3 SMALL EGGPLANTS

SALT

⅔ CUP VIRGIN OLIVE OIL

1 ONION, THINLY SLICED

1 RED SWEET PEPPER, SEEDED AND THINLY SLICED

2 CLOVES GARLIC, CRUSHED

2 TOMATOES, FINELY CHOPPED

2 TABLESPOONS CHOPPED FRESH CILANTRO

2 TEASPOONS PAPRIKA

1 TEASPOON GROUND CUMIN

½ TEASPOON GROUND ALLSPICE

1 TABLESPOON LEMON JUICE

4 TABLESPOONS TOMATO PASTE

PINCH OF SUGAR

SALT AND PEPPER

===

◇ Cut a deep slice along the whole length of each eggplant and sprinkle in plenty of salt. Set aside.
◇ Heat 3 tablespoons oil in a frying pan and sauté the onion, pepper and garlic for 10 minutes. Add the tomatoes, cilantro, spices, lemon juice, tomato paste, sugar and seasonings and simmer for 5 minutes.
◇ Wash out the eggplants and dry thoroughly. Heat the remaining oil in a large frying pan and fry the eggplants for 5 minutes, until lightly browned on all sides. Remove with a slotted spoon and cool slightly.
◇ Place the eggplants in a baking dish, slit sides up. Carefully open the slits and fill with the onion mixture, spooning any extra filling into the dish. Pour in 1 cup boiling water and bake in a preheated oven at 400°F for 1 hour.
◇ Remove from the oven and chill. Refrigerate until ready to serve and cut the eggplants into thick slices.
◇ Serve with yogurt and plenty of bread.

LEFT *Spiced chicken with tabbouleh molds*
RIGHT *Oven-baked eggplant salad*

PORK MEDLEY

~

These stuffed pork tenderloins are served on a bed of marinated white kidney beans and sweet peppers. It is a wonderful medley of flavors, colors and textures, and a mouth-watering supper dish.

══

2 RED SWEET PEPPERS

1 CUP WHITE KIDNEY BEANS, SOAKED
OVERNIGHT

BOUQUET GARNI

1 CLOVE GARLIC, PEELED

1 TEASPOON CUMIN SEEDS

1 TEASPOON CORIANDER SEEDS

1 DRIED RED CHILLI, DE-SEEDED

1 BAYLEAF

6 WHOLE PEPPERCORNS

A SMALL PIECE CHEESECLOTH

2 12-OUNCE PORK TENDERLOINS

STUFFING

3 APRICOTS, PITTED AND FINELY CHOPPED

⅓ CUP TOASTED AND FINELY CHOPPED
CASHEW NUTS

1 TABLESPOON CHOPPED FRESH SAGE

1 TABLESPOON CHOPPED FRESH PARSLEY

PINCH OF GROUND CUMIN

A LITTLE BEATEN EGG TO BIND

DRESSING

⅔ CUP OLIVE OIL

JUICE OF 2 LEMONS

1 CLOVE GARLIC, CRUSHED

1 TEASPOON PAPRIKA

½ TEASPOON GROUND CUMIN

SALT AND PEPPER

TO GARNISH

LEMON WEDGES

CHOPPED FRESH PARSLEY AND PARSLEY
SPRIGS

══

◇ Place the peppers under a hot broiler and cook until the skins are charred and blistered. Tie in a plastic bag and chill.

◇ Drain the soaked beans and place in a large saucepan. Cover with cold water. Tie the bouquet garni ingredients in the cheesecloth and add to the pan. Bring to a boil, boil rapidly for 10 minutes, lower the heat and simmer, uncovered, for 40-45 minutes until the beans are cooked.

◇ Prepare the pork: wash and dry the tenderloins and split open along 1 side, but do not cut through. Open them out flat and season well. Combine the stuffing ingredients together, adding enough beaten egg to bind the mixture.

◇ Divide the stuffing between the 2 tenderloins, spreading it down the center of each one. Close the sides of the pork over the filling and tie firmly with string, at 1-inch intervals, along each tenderloin.

◇ Place the tenderloins in a roasting pan and cook in a preheated oven at 400°F for 40 minutes. Remove from the oven and chill until completely cold.

◇ Peel and seed the cooked peppers over a bowl to catch any juices. Cut the peppers into thin strips.

◇ Blend the dressing ingredients into the pepper juices.

◇ Drain the cooked beans and discard the bouquet garni. Place in a large bowl and pour in the dressing. Toss well and leave until cold. Stir in the peppers and transfer to a large serving dish.

◇ Remove the string from the cold pork and cut into thick slices. Lay the slices over the marinated beans and peppers and garnish with the lemon wedges, chopped parsley and parsley sprigs.

Pork medley

SALMON & SOLE CEVICHE

~

Adapted from an authentic Samoan recipe, this dish of marinated fish, served with a coconut sauce, is pure delight.

═══

12 OUNCES SALMON FILLETS, SKINNED

12 OUNCES SOLE FILLETS, SKINNED

MARINADE

JUICE OF 4 LIMES

5 TABLESPOONS OLIVE OIL

1 TEASPOON SESAME OIL

GRATED RIND OF 2 LIMES

3-INCH PIECE LEMON GRASS, CRUSHED OR GRATED RIND OF 1 LEMON

2 SCALLIONS, TRIMMED AND THICKLY SLICED

4 SPRIGS FRESH CILANTRO, BRUISED

1 TEASPOON CORIANDER SEEDS, BRUISED

1 SMALL GREEN CHILLI PEPPER, SEEDED AND SLICED

PINCH OF SUGAR

SAUCE

⅓ CUP CREAM OF COCONUT

A FEW SHREDDED CILANTRO LEAVES

PINCH OF CAYENNE PEPPER

SALT AND PEPPER

═══

◇ Remove any small bones from the salmon. Slice the salmon and sole fillets thinly, and place in a shallow dish.
◇ Blend together the lime juice, olive oil and sesame oil and pour over the fish. Add the remaining marinade ingredients to the dish, cover and marinate for 2 hours in the refrigerator, turning the fish from time to time.
◇ Remove the fish, cover and keep cool. Strain the marinade into a small pan, add the coconut and heat gently, to boiling. Remove from the heat and cool.
◇ Stir in the cilantro leaves and cayenne. Season.
◇ Serve the marinated fish with a spoonful of sauce and a salad garnish.

B.L.T. SALAD

~

Crispy bacon, lettuce and cherry tomatoes make a tasty and attractive salad.

═══

4 OUNCES BACON,

2 TABLESPOONS BUTTER

4 SLICES WHITE BREAD, CRUSTS REMOVED AND CUBED

1 SMALL BABY ENDIVE

1 SMALL COS LETTUCE

1 SMALL AVOCADO

6 OUNCES MOZZARELLA CHEESE, CUBED

12 CHERRY TOMATOES, HALVED

DRESSING

½ CUP EXTRA VIRGIN OLIVE OIL

2 TABLESPOONS WHITE WINE VINEGAR

¼ TEASPOON CHILLI POWDER

SALT

═══

◇ Dice the bacon and stir-fry over a high heat until crisp and golden. Remove with a slotted spoon and drain on paper towels.
◇ Add the butter to the pan and stir-fry the cubed bread until crisp and golden. Drain on paper towels.
◇ Wash and dry the lettuces, discarding any tough outer leaves and tear into bite-size pieces. Peel, pit and slice the avocado and add to the bowl with the mozzarella and tomatoes.
◇ Blend the dressing ingredients together and pour over the salad. Toss well and serve at once.

FRONT *Salmon & sole ceviche*
BACK *B.L.T. salad*

TIRAMISU WITH RASPBERRIES

~

This is my version of the Italian cream cheese pudding Tiramisu. This recipe serves 8 – 10.

════

ALMOND FINGERS

3 EGGS

⅓ CUP SUPERFINE SUGAR

½ CUP GROUND ALMONDS

1½ TABLESPOONS ALL-PURPOSE FLOUR

2 TABLESPOONS UNSALTED BUTTER, MELTED

8 OUNCES RASPBERRIES

⅔ CUP STRONG BLACK COFFEE

1 TABLESPOON BRANDY

3 TABLESPOONS DARK RUM

1½ CUPS MASCARPONE (OR CREAM) CHEESE

2 TABLESPOONS SUGAR

2 EGGS, SEPARATED

TOPPING

3 TABLESPOONS COCOA POWDER

½ SQUARE DARK CHOCOLATE, GRATED

════

◇ Beat the eggs and sugar together in a bowl over a pan of simmering water, until thick and pale, about 10 minutes. Fold in the almonds, flour and butter until combined and pour into a greased and lined 9×13-inch baking pan. Smooth the surface.

◇ Bake in a preheated oven at 375°F for 12-15 minutes, until risen and golden. Turn out and cool on a wire rack. Carefully peel away the baking paper and cut the sponge into 12 large fingers. Place in a large shallow dish and sprinkle the raspberries over.

◇ Mix together the coffee, brandy and 2 tablespoons of the rum, and pour over the sponge and raspberries.

◇ Beat together the mascarpone, remaining rum, sugar and egg yolks. Whisk the whites until stiff, fold into the mixture and spoon over the sponge. Sift over the cocoa powder, top with grated chocolate and chill for 2 hours.

GINGERBREAD

~

Although this quantity makes a large cake, it keeps very well wrapped in a double layer of foil and stored in a cool place. You'll have no trouble finishing off any leftovers!

════

1⅓ CUPS BROWN SUGAR

¾ CUP UNSALTED BUTTER

⅔ CUP MOLASSES

⅔ CUP CORN SYRUP

3 CUPS SELF-RISING FLOUR

1¼ CUPS COCONUT

2 TEASPOONS GROUND GINGER

½ TEASPOON BAKING SODA

½ TEASPOON SALT

1¼ CUPS MILK

1 EGG, LIGHTLY BEATEN

TO SERVE

FRESH APRICOTS

CRÈME FRAÎCHE

════

◇ Grease and line the base and sides of a 7×11-inch baking pan.

◇ Heat the sugar, butter, molasses and corn syrup together in a pan, until melted.

◇ Combine the flour, coconut, ginger, baking soda and salt in a large bowl. Make a well in the center and beat in the melted syrup mixture, milk and egg, until combined. Continue to beat for 1 minute.

◇ Pour into the prepared pan and bake in a preheated oven at 350°F for 1¼-1½ hours, or until a skewer inserted in the center comes out clean.

◇ Cool in the pan for 10 minutes, turn out on to a rack and let cool.

◇ Serve cut into fingers with apricots and crème fraîche.

CENTER AND RIGHT *Tiramisu with raspberries*
LEFT *Gingerbread*

PLUM, SAUTERN & CINNAMON ICE-CREAM

~

Sauterne is a delicious dessert wine making this a fragrant and refreshingly different ice-cream.

═══

1 POUND PLUMS

⅔ CUP SAUTERNE

SCANT 2 CUPS MILK

2 CINNAMON STICKS

6 EGG YOLKS

½ CUP SUPERFINE SUGAR

⅔ CUP HEAVY OR WHIPPING CREAM

TO SERVE

3 PLUMS, HALVED, PITTED AND SLICED

A LITTLE EXTRA SAUTERNE (OPTIONAL)

═══

◇ Halve and pit the plums and place in a saucepan. Add the wine and bring to a boil, cover and simmer gently for 5 minutes, until the plums are tender. Purée until smooth and cool.

◇ Scald the milk with the cinnamon, infuse for 10 minutes, and strain.

◇ Beat the egg yolks and sugar together until pale and creamy, pour in the milk, beating all the time, and pass through a fine sieve into a clean pan. Heat gently, stirring, until the mixture thickens and coats the back of the spoon. Do not let the custard boil or it will curdle. Remove from the heat and leave to go cold.

◇ Combine the fruit purée and custard. Lightly whip the cream and fold into the mixture. Place in a plastic container and transfer to the freezer.

◇ Freeze for 3-4 hours, beating well every hour or so to prevent ice crystals forming.

◇ Remove the ice-cream from the freezer 15 minutes before serving, to allow it to soften slightly. Scoop into dishes and serve topped with fresh plum slices and a little Sauterne if desired.

SPICED BRAISED PEARS

~

In this refreshing and light summer dessert the pears are braised with red wine, port and spices and served chilled, with ice-cream or cream.

═══

¾ CUP SUPERFINE SUGAR

SCANT 1 CUP DRY RED WINE

⅔ CUP WATER

2 TABLESPOONS PORT

4 STRIPS LEMON PEEL

JUICE OF 1 LEMON

2 CINNAMON STICKS

6 WHOLE CLOVES

6 MEDIUM EATING PEARS

TO SERVE

VANILLA ICE-CREAM

WHIPPED CREAM

═══

◇ Place all the ingredients, except the pears, in a large pan. Heat gently until the sugar is dissolved.

◇ Peel the pears leaving the stalk in place and add to the pan. Bring the liquid just to boiling point, cover and simmer over a very low heat for 35-40 minutes, turning the pears frequently. Do not allow the liquid to boil or the pears will become mushy.

◇ Transfer the pears to a serving dish and pour over the liquid. Refrigerate until well chilled.

◇ Serve the pears with ice-cream or whipped cream, whichever you prefer.

RIGHT *Plum, Sauterne & cinnamon ice-cream*
LEFT *Spiced braised pears*

CITRUS ICE-CREAM SHERBET

~

Freshly squeezed grapefruit and orange juice is served with a scoop of vanilla ice-cream, and topped with soda water, for a delicious non-alcoholic fruit sherbet.

2 CUPS FRESHLY SQUEEZED GRAPEFRUIT
JUICE

2 CUPS FRESHLY SQUEEZED ORANGE JUICE

6 SCOOPS VANILLA ICE-CREAM

2 CUPS CHILLED SODA WATER

◇ Blend the fruit juices together and pour into 6 large tumblers.

◇ Add a scoop of ice-cream to each glass, fill glass with the soda water and serve immediately.

ICED MOCHA COFFEE

~

A deliciously rich chocolate-flavored iced coffee – perfect for a hot summer day. This drink should be served as chilled as possible.

4 CUPS BOILING WATER

6 TABLESPOONS GROUND MEDIUM ROAST
COFFEE

3 SQUARES DARK CHOCOLATE, GRATED

3-4 TABLESPOONS SUPERFINE SUGAR

TO SERVE

MILK OR LIGHT CREAM

◇ Pour the boiling water over coffee in a cafetière or large heat-proof carafe and allow to infuse for 10 minutes.

◇ Either plunge the stopper or pour the coffee through a fine sieve and stir in the chocolate and sugar until dissolved. Let cool and refrigerate for several hours or overnight.

◇ Remove from the refrigerator just before serving, stir well and pass through a fine sieve.

◇ Divide between 6 large tumblers and top with the milk or cream to taste.

CHAMPAGNE SUNSET

~

This delicious champagne cocktail is loosely based on a tequila sunrise. It makes the perfect aperitif for a warm summer evening.

1¼ CUPS FRESHLY SQUEEZED ORANGE JUICE

6 TABLESPOONS COINTREAU

1 BOTTLE CHILLED CHAMPAGNE

GRENADINE

◇ Blend the orange juice and Cointreau together and divide between 6 champagne flutes.

◇ Fill with champagne, add a dash of grenadine to each glass and serve immediately.

BACK LEFT *Citrus ice-cream sherbet*
FRONT *Iced mocha coffee*
BACK RIGHT *Champagne sunset*

INDEX

A

Apple and blueberry muffins, spiced 82
Apricot and pistachio pie 56
Avocado dip with crudités, summer 10

B

Bacon:
Bacon and banana kabobs 46
Bacon and mushroom pie 16
Sausage, bacon and apricot kabobs 20
Bananas:
Bacon and banana kabobs 46
Foiled rum bananas 54
Beef and herb roulade 78
Beef and vegetable kabobs with herby yogurt sauce 44
Beet, tarragon and ginger salad 70
B.L.T. salad 102

C

Caramelized oranges 80
Carrot and zucchini salad 18
Champagne sunset 108
Cheese (savory):
Cos salad with blue brie dressing 16
Feta, walnut and onion dip 66
Gorgonzola and asparagus quiche 70
Radicchio with broiled chèvre cheese 90
Cheese (sweet):
Ricotta, nut and honey cheese 30
Strawberry cheese with shortbread 28
Tiramisu with raspberries 104
Cheesecake with summer berry sauce, lemon 82
Chicken:
Chicken liver pâté 20
Country chicken, ham and herb terrine 74

Persian chicken kabobs 38
Southern chicken wings with spicy barbecue sauce 42
Spiced chicken with tabbouleh molds 98
Chinese spiced riblets 46
Citrus ice-cream sherbet 108
Cos salad with blue brie dressing 16
Crab and mango phyllo pastries 64
Cucumber soup, iced 12
Curried eggs 14

D

Desserts:
Apricot and pistachio pie 56
Caramelized oranges 80
Foiled rum bananas 54
Fruit kabobs with honey glaze 54
Lemon cheesecake with summer berry sauce 82
Peach and cinnamon puffs 56
Pear and cardamom tatin 80
Plum, Sauterne and cinnamon ice-cream 106
Refrigerator cake 30
Ricotta, nut and honey cheese 30
Spiced braised pears 106
Strawberry cheese with shortbread 28
Summer berry fool 28
Tiramisu with raspberries 104
Dolmades 66
Drinks:
Blushing strawberry fizz 58
Champagne sunset 108
Citrus ice-cream sherbet 108
Homemade lemonade 58
Iced mocha coffee 108
Orchard bloom 32
Peach nectar 84
Pink peril 32
Raspberry and ginger cordial 84
Sangria 58
Southern mint julep 84
Sparkling fruit cup 32

E

Eggplant pâté 14
Eggplant salad, oven-baked 98

Eggs:
Curried 14
Spinach tortilla 18
Thai-style shrimp 64

F

Feta, walnut and onion dip 66
Fish (see also Seafood):
Pan-fried fish steaks 50
Red mullet with fennel 40
Salmon and dill flan 72
Salmon and sole ceviche 102
Smoked salmon phyllo tartlets 88
Smoked salmon 'sausages' 12
Smoked trout paste 72
Tuna fish saté 50
Watercress roulade with smoked haddock 96
Fruit cup, sparkling 32
Fruit kabobs with honey glaze 54

G

Garlic:
Moroccan spiced garlic bread 36
Tomato and olive oil bruschetta 40
Gingerbread 104
Gorgonzola and asparagus quiche 70

K

Kabobs:
Bacon and banana 46
Beef and vegetable with herby yogurt sauce 44
Fruit with honey glaze 54
Persian chicken 38
Sausage, bacon and apricot 20
Shrimp and monkfish with coconut salsa 38

L

Lamb cutlets, minted 68
Lamb steaks, glazed 42
Leeks à la Grecque 24
Lemon cheesecake with summer berry sauce 82
Lemonade, homemade 58
Lentil and cashew nut soup 36

M

Melon and mint soup, chilled   10

Mint julep, southern   84

Mocha coffee, iced   108

Moroccan spiced garlic bread   36

Muffins, spiced apple and blueberry   82

Mushrooms, foil-baked   52

O

Onion and pepper relish   78

Onions with sun-dried tomatoes, stuffed   94

Orchard bloom   32

Oranges, caramelized   80

P

Pasta:

Pasta, ham and apricot salad   68

Pasta salad with tuna sauce   22

Warm pasta pommodoro   94

Pastry:

Apricot and pistachio tart   56

Bacon and mushroom pie   16

Crab and mango phyllo pastries   64

Gorgonzola and asparagus quiche   70

Peach and cinnamon puffs   56

Pear and cardamom tatin   80

Smoked salmon phyllo tartlets   88

Pâtés:

Chicken liver   20

Eggplant   14

Pea and lettuce soup, fresh   88

Peach and cinnamon puffs   56

Peach nectar   84

Pear and cardamom tatin   80

Pears, spiced braised   106

Peppers, broiled   48

Pink peril   32

Pissaladière   76

Plum, Sauterne and cinnamon ice-cream   106

Pork:

Chinese spiced riblets   46

Pork medley   100

Prosciutto salad   90

R

Radicchio with broiled chèvre cheese   90

Raspberry and ginger cordial   84

Red mullet with fennel   40

Refrigerator cake   30

Ricotta, nut and honey cheese   30

S

Salade Niçoise   24

Salads:

Beet, tarragon and ginger   70

B.L.T.   102

Carrot and zucchini   18

Cos with blue brie dressing   16

Oven-baked eggplant   98

Pasta, ham and apricot   68

Pasta with tuna sauce   22

Prosciutto   90

Salade Niçoise   24

Sicilian potato   26

Summer greens   74

Three bean   26

Salmon and dill pie   72

Salmon and sole ceviche   102

Sangria   58

Sausage, bacon and apricot kabobs   20

Scallop and mussel escabeche   92

Seafood:

Crab and mango phyllo pastries   64

Scallop and mussel escabeche   92

Shrimp and monkfish kabobs with coconut salsa   38

Thai-style shrimp eggs   64

Sicilian potato salad   26

Smoked salmon phyllo tartlets   88

Smoked salmon 'sausages'   12

Smoked trout paste   72

Soups:

Chilled melon and mint   10

Fresh pea and lettuce   88

Iced cucumber   12

Lentil and cashew nut   36

Watercress and herb   62

Spinach and ricotta pie   96

Spinach tortilla   18

Stilton with port and pear, potted   62

Strawberry cheese with shortbread   28

Strawberry fizz, blushing   58

Summer berry fool   28

Summer greens salad   74

Sweet potatoes, baked, with garlic and thyme   52

T

Thai-style shrimp eggs   64

Three bean salad   26

Tiramisu with raspberries   104

Tomato and olive oil bruschetta   40

Trout paste, smoked   72

V

Vegetables:

Baked sweet potatoes with garlic and thyme   52

Broiled peppers   48

Foil-baked mushrooms   52

Leeks à la Grecque   24

Sesame zucchini   48

Stuffed onions with sun-=dried tomatoes   94

W

Watercress and herb soup   62

Watercress and salmon rolls   22

Watercress roulade with smoked haddock   96

Z

Zucchini:

Carrot and zucchini salad   18

Sesame zucchini   48

ACKNOWLEDGMENTS

~

The publishers would like to thank the following for
their help in the preparation of this book:

Alison Leach for the index

Mary Talbot for use of The Old Farm

For picnicware and fabrics:

Brats Ltd
281 King's Road
London SW3

Ian Mankin Ltd
109 Regent's Park Road
London NW1

Antoinette Putnam
55 Regent's Park Road
London NW1